CORPORATE STRESS

Corporate Stress

Rosalind Forbes, Ed.D.

A Dolphin Book
DOUBLEDAY & COMPANY, INC.
GARDEN CITY, NEW YORK
1979

ISBN: 0-385-14440-7
Library of Congress Catalog Card Number 78–55849

To my family
my thanks
for your love, help, understanding, and patience

CONTENTS

PREFACE

Everyone who works knows that on-the-job pressure is one of the major sources of stress in daily life. Deadlines, emergencies, day-to-day relationships with peers, subordinates, and bosses have a way of creeping into the Monday-to-Friday life of workers at all levels of income and responsibility.

This book is not intended to show you how to eliminate pressure from the job. For one thing, not all job-related stress is the result of too much to do in too little time. Some people suffer as much from stress underload, which is the debilitating boredom of not having enough interesting things to do, as others do from stress overload.

What we start with in this book are clues to help you identify your own particular sources of stress, whether they are in the nature of your responsibilities, in your working relationships, or even in your personality structure. You can learn to live with stress, to manage it and find a level where it will work to enhance your productivity and job satisfaction rather than diminish it. There is an optimal stress level for every person in every job.

Special attention is given to the problems of managers, working women, and members of certain high-stress occupations.

Finally, specific questionnaires are directed at you to help you pinpoint your own stresses. Throughout the book there are also a variety of techniques to help you manage stress on both personal and interpersonal levels.

Stress is not necessarily negative. Without it, sales campaigns would never get off the ground, reports would never get written or distributed, no one would ever get to work on time. But it is a powerful force, capable of spawning killer diseases, and it must be understood and managed if it is to be a source of power. This book contains the means to that success.

CORPORATE STRESS

STRESS AND JOB PERFORMANCE

Physical, Mental, and Emotional Stress

Stress often evokes physical, mental, and emotional reactions to situations that cause fear, uncertainty, danger, excitement, irritation, confusion, or change.

All stress is not the same; therefore it does not always cause similar reactions. The signs of physical stress are usually visible and easily attended to. If you break your leg or catch the flu, it is easy to see that your body is under physical stress. Rushing to catch a bus or train, running up a flight of stairs, overexposure to cold or heat, pulling a muscle or going through surgery, all cause physical stress.

Physical stress is not inherently positive or negative; much depends upon the quantity of stress and the manner in which it is created. While sustaining a bodily injury may be classified as negative physical stress, indulging in the right amount of aerobic or calisthenic exercises provides a positive physical stress.

Often, an illness that appears to be physical may actually stem from mental or emotional causes. A headache right before an unpleasant meeting may be an unconscious protest against attending. An ulcer developed during a difficult transition between jobs may really indicate unhappiness with the situation or anxiety caused by lack of confidence.

In the same way, strong emotions can produce bodily changes. Anger, for example, creates tension. This emotion causes hormones to speed through your body, producing a number of physical reactions: your heart will beat more rapidly, your stomach muscles will contract, and your blood pressure will rise.

The mind, body, and emotions are not the separate entities they were once thought to be. They are one integral unit. One affects the other, sometimes in a positive way and sometimes in a negative way.

Stress generally becomes detrimental only when it is prolonged beyond what an individual can comfortably handle. And, whether we like it or not, a certain amount of stress is simply inevitable.

New York's Life Extension Institute recently conducted a study of its clients to determine the degree of stress related to job security, family problems, and personal habits like drinking and smoking. The results were compared with those of a 1958 study and indicated stress had indeed risen dangerously in the last two decades.

Many business people deal with these stresses in different ways. It is not unusual any more to find high-powered, successful executives "dropping out" and buying farms in Vermont. Nor is it unusual to find a stockbroker turning house painter or a pilot moving to Europe to become a tour guide. When questioned, they will often say they did it because the pressures of their old job "weren't worth it."

Others are opting for early retirement at age fifty-five rather than continue to face the pressures of a demanding job. They may have successfully moved up in careers which involved responsibility for large staffs of people and huge sums of money, but by then they would rather not have to fight the competition. They often plateau out or develop a neurotic suspicion that every subordinate is competing for their jobs.

This suspicion of job competition is partly based on the facts of life in the corporate hierarchy. As one begins to rise within the corporate structure, the demands on the individual become greater and more is expected in terms of company loyalty. Peers may become subordinates. Responsibility for people and the pressure to produce definable results increases threefold. A manager may be caught in the vise of conflicting demands: demands from above to get more done with fewer people, and demands from below requesting additional help.

It is not unusual to find the "Peter Principle" as the cause of stress when an employee is promoted to a position which is beyond his capabilities. As the work becomes too difficult to handle, insecurities in his talents and flaws in his self-image develop, and this lack of confidence further affects his work and increases stress.

Other sources of mental stress are related to work overload and job insecurity. These pressures increase as you move up the corporate hierarchy. Additionally, there are the burdens that go along with decision-making and the isolation of the leadership role.

As long as an individual remains a part of an organization there is little that can be done to change job stress. To change the stress, the organizational system itself would have to be changed. Instead you have to change your reactions to stress areas.

Emotional stress can be positive as well as negative. It can give you a zest for life and pep in your work. Without emotions we would become little more than robots.

It is only negative emotions which are bottled up inside us that present health problems; the emotions themselves are neutral factors. The stress that harms is the stress that comes from fear or frustration, from continued anxiety or persistent anger. When these emotions are hosted by us on a continued basis, they may create a multitude of medical problems.

One research project which showed the relationship between emotional stress and illness took as its subjects about a thousand women of the same age, training, and income. Approximately one third of these women had a work absentee rate and illness record four times higher than that of their peers. Closer observation indicated that the sicker women had measurably more frustrations, worries, and difficulties in their lives than the balance of the test group. They tended to be widows and divorcees who still had small children to care for. Their lives were generally filled with disappointment and insecurity.

A similar study of men in comparable working conditions found that one third of the group had seventy-five per cent of the illnesses. The reason was determined to be emotional stress brought on by illness in the family, problems with children, financial worries, unhappy marriages, or frustrations in career advancement. It is situations like these that cause anger, depression, and discouragement.

Whenever one's goals or strivings are blocked by obstacles seemingly beyond control, frustration is experienced. Inflation, discrimination, or loss of a loved one all present external frustrations. Lack of competence in fulfilling one's job, inadequate self-control, and other similar limitations of personal resources pose internal frustration.

Conflict is a type of frustration that occurs when we must choose one alternative in place of something else. It results from having to choose between two needs or goals of equal importance. Taking one job, for example, may mean turning down another that seems equally desirable, or it may mean relocating to a city you don't like. The conflict will be at its peak when you are trying to make up your mind; once the decision is reached, stress is diminished.

A type of emotional stress which is even more subtle results from pressure to accomplish particular career goals, or from constraints which demand behavior or actions in harmony with predetermined role expectations. A business person may submit to pressures like entertaining clients or taking on extra projects at work in order to be considered for a promotion. A minister's child may sit quietly through long meetings when he would really prefer to participate in weekend Little League games.

Pressure, regardless of the source, forces a person to quicken the pace of his lifestyle. It may cause him to intensify his dedication to a career or a project completion, and it may even motivate him to change goals.

Stress is a part of every working day and can usually be handled without difficulty. Excessive pressures, however, can be emotionally draining.

Physical, mental, and emotional stress are seldom isolated from one another. There is a complex interaction that continuously changes the effects of one upon the other. Knowing this, and knowing how and where to look for the cause of such stress, is the first step toward successfully managing job stress.

Learning to Live with Stress

A change in behavior and attitude can decidedly affect your ability to cope and live with stress.

1. APPRAISE THE SITUATION to determine the type and intensity of the stress. If the pressure is perceived as a career threat, coping with the emotional worry of it will likely interrupt your ongoing work performance. To avoid this, realize what is likely to happen if anyone ever does threaten your job and then you won't be thrown off guard when and if it does happen. Pinpointing the source of stress will make it easier to deal with the situation, especially if you have had a similar problem in the past.

2. HAVE SEVERAL ALTERNATIVE COURSES OF ACTION OR BEHAVIOR PLANNED once you have appraised the situation. Then assess the merits of each solution and choose the one which is most viable. Your decision should be based on which action has the best probability of success as well as on the amount of time or energy you are willing to expend and the level of satisfaction you are likely to receive. This involves balancing probability, cost, and desirability.

3. PUT FORTH THE EFFORT TO PUT YOUR DECISION INTO ACTION. After taking action, use feedback from your environment to see what adjustments or changes may be necessary. Be prepared for the possibility that you may decide to terminate one course of action and implement another.

4. THE WORST TIME TO MAKE ANY DECISION IS WHEN YOU ARE EMOTIONALLY UPSET or pressured by time or people. If you do make a decision at a time like this, you are likely to make more errors in judgment than you normally would.

5. RECOGNIZE THE PRESSURES ASSOCIATED WITH THE LEADERSHIP ROLE. These include decision-making, overwork, and job insecurity. The demands of a responsible position may occasionally require brief periods of time off to relieve the mental strain. Be prepared to take from seventy-two to ninety-six hours off from work whenever you feel the pressure becoming unmanageable.

6. Remember, EXPOSURE TO STRESS HELPS YOU BUILD UP A CERTAIN AMOUNT OF IMMUNITY. The more you allow yourself to be exposed to pressure, the less disturbing your emotional reactions will become. In fact, they will also become less frequent. However, building this immunity requires a knowledge of how you are affected by specific stressful conditions. If you are criticized for poor job performance, for example, it may be that stress will inhibit you from improving. Or it may be that stress caused you to do poorly in the first place. Failure to realize this may

cause you to overreact to the criticism and even lose your objectivity.

7. REALIZE IT IS NOT HUMANLY POSSIBLE TO REMOVE STRESS FROM YOUR LIFE OR FREE YOURSELF FROM REACTING TO IT. Everyone has his own stress threshold beyond which behavior and performance diminish. Defining and recognizing your own threshold can help you take steps to avoid going beyond it.

8. AVOID THINKING OR DISCUSSING BUSINESS DURING LUNCH OR BREAK TIME. Try to separate yourself completely from work during what are supposed to be rest times. Some people feel this takes time and performance away from their job endeavors, and they often prefer to work through lunch or elective break times. In actuality, it has been positively proven that workers produce better amounts and quality of work after short breaks. Briefly freeing your mind of work problems facilitates your maintenance of personal balance and perspective.

9. TALK WITH A FRIEND OR CONFIDANT as a way of relieving stress. Verbalizing problems helps clarify your thoughts and gives you an objective perspective on the situation. Just the act of talking will in itself reduce tension.

10. USE THE SAME ORGANIZED APPROACH IN YOUR PERSONAL LIFE THAT YOU USE AT WORK. Schedule time and activities with friends and family. Capitalize on your administrative skills to combat stress and handle personal problems.

How Optimal Stress Can Enhance Productivity and Give You That Competitive Edge

All cameras focus on the Olympic diver as he warms up. His muscles taut, he paces up and down while gulping air and shaking his arms. Keyed up by the stress of competition, his entire body is in a state of tense readiness for the immediate task ahead.

He concentrates intensely on the dive, completely oblivious to all the excitement around him. Spectators follow his every move as he steps on the diving board almost twelve yards above the water. Diving from that height, he will hit water at thirty-five miles an hour.

Tension is near the breaking point for the diver and spectators alike. A silent hush fills the stadium as he prepares to dive.

The athlete dashes forward, jumps off the high board to do three and a half flips, and hits the water like an arrow. It is a perfect dive, a fitting climax and reward for the months and years when he prepared four to six hours every day so he would be ready for this very event.

The diver has learned through trial and error to find his optimal level of stress. By channeling this delicate balance of tension, he is able to utilize it for top performance.

A sales manager prepares to lead his company's national sales meeting. His pulse quickens and there is a fluttering feeling in his stomach as he readies himself for the talk. In the past he would have tried to bolster his confidence with one or two martinis, or even with a tranquilizer, but though they reduced tension they also reduced his mental alertness.

Although he can feel the tension mounting, he is still confident and in control of the situation. Experience has taught him that the right amount of stress can actually give him that extra push which makes the difference between superior and mediocre performance.

He is not afraid of the tension. In fact, he welcomes it.

In the few minutes before his presentation, he glances at his audience. Most of the top brass in the company are there. Everything he says will be weighed carefully. There is a great deal at stake, and he realizes it.

The salesman prepares himself by reviewing the presentation in his mind. This gives him a "psychological set" which results in maximum concentration.

As he gets up to speak, his entire body becomes tense. His blood pressure rises slightly, his palms are sweaty, and adrenalin pours into his blood stream to give him extra energy. He feels somewhat anxious, but the stress of the situation energizes him into a state of tense readiness.

As he begins to speak, he notices that his words are flowing smoothly. Memory, recall, and concentration are razor keen. He swiftly gains the interest and attention of his audience. People are nodding and smiling by the time he makes his closing remarks, and a round of applause follows as he sits down.

The talk is over. He lets out a sigh and begins to "come down," feeling good about his performance. Within an hour he is relaxed and calm again.

The Olympic diver and the sales manager have both discovered the secret of converting stress into productive energy. Each has learned how much tension he can tolerate without breaking. He has also learned the amount of stress necessary for him to perform at his best.

When you work at optimal stress level you are aware of an exhilaration you would not experience if you were not under pressure. If you allow yourself to go beyond that level, you will become less productive, but if you are below that level you will probably not produce at peak performance or experience your full potential for satisfaction in your accomplishment. In fact, if you allow yourself to exist too far below your optimal stress level, you will actually vegetate.

Every individual has his own optimal stress level. He obtains the key to top performance when he determines what that level is.

Successful business people thrive on a certain amount of stress. It provides them with that extra drive which stimulates motivation and achievement.

Anyone in sales or marketing knows that without the tension of quotas and deadlines the job would lose the challenge and excitement that spurs them on to productive effort.

A survey of nine hundred executives revealed that those who were the least afraid of challenges or pressures in their lives appeared to be more successful than the group who avoided stress-inducing situations. The latter group either failed or simply did not move up in their jobs.

Stress prepares one for peak performance. When working at an optimal tension level, one actually is more productive.

An interview of one hundred and twenty men and

women asked for their descriptions of peak and average performance. The results of the study indicated that one of the prime ingredients for peak performance is the ability to focus all one's attention on the task at hand. Most people work while simultaneously losing mental energy to other distractions, whether those distractions be background music, a nagging headache, or even a conversation in another room. However, peak performance is achieved only when the performer has learned to focus on the one activity at hand and totally ignore any background distractions.

Scientists have long known that tension produces a heightening of attention that helps people perform better and learn more quickly. This increased stress motivates the body to mobilize and sharpen all its mental and physical functions, from readying muscles for instant action to alerting the sense organs to be more acute. In fact, the stress even improves the ability of the central nervous system to analyze and process incoming information.

Mental acuity and the ability to view problems objectively are essential to anyone in a decision-making position. This type of mental activity, however, depends on the individual's ability to direct available mental energy toward the completion of a single task.

Intense concentration produces changes in brain waves. In response to challenging or novel problems, the brain produces additional high-frequency brain waves. Ordinarily we use beta brain waves, at fourteen to twenty-one cycles per second, to get most jobs done. When solving more complex problems, gamma waves of forty cycles per second begin to materialize.

This focusing of attention on one task is necessary if the

brain is to process information adequately. In Western society, the left hemisphere of the brain is predominant because it is the hemisphere which deals with logical, analytical, verbal, and mathematical abilities. It operates in a linear, sequential fashion. The left brain processes only one piece of information at a time. When too much stress or stimulus is presented at once, the higher cortical functions of the brain cannot operate properly and the ability to think and reason are consequently reduced. This is why a person under excessive stress will tend to make more mistakes and errors in judgment than would be normal for him under conditions of no stress overload.

In addition to improved accuracy of judgment and clarity of perception, the person who works at optimal stress level will experience a high amount of flexibility and improved energy flow. The stress will motivate him to a high level of activity and he will be able to work long hours without tiring.

The individual working at optimal stress level will generally maintain composure during crisis situations, even if all others in the group are losing control. He will also be able easily to generate new strategies and alternatives if things do not go as planned.

Optimal stress level is characterized by relaxed control under pressure, an optimistic outlook, heightened perceptual awareness, and a surge of energy. One of the best ways to determine whether you are working at this optimal level is to note how quickly you can relax and release tension after the completion of a job. If it takes more than a few hours for you to achieve a relaxed state, you are working beyond your optimal stress level.

Are You Working at Optimal Stress Level?

Here is a checklist to help you recognize whether you are using stress to your advantage:

Check those statements which generally apply to you.

1. _____ I feel exhilarated after completing an important business deal or project.

2. _____ Stress helps me to be more alert and to think clearly and perceptively.

3. _____ I am able to "come down" physically and emotionally just a few hours after the termination of a stressful situation.

4. _____ The stress I experience is rarely prolonged or severe.

5. _____ I am able to stay calm and work productively under pressure.

6. _____ I can accept setbacks and interruptions without emotional letdowns.

7. _____ I approach problems with flexibility and seek to generate several alternative solutions.

8. _____ I generally view problems objectively and realistically.

9. _____ Stress increases my motivation and drive.

10. _____ I know how to channel stress into productive work.

If you checked seven out of ten items, the stress you live and work under is right for you and enhances your performance. If you checked five or six statements, you get the job done but you are likely to feel tired afterward. And if you responded to only four or less of the items, stress is likely to limit your effectiveness.

Why Stress Underload and Overload Decrease Job Effectiveness

A national newspaper once carried a front-page article about an official of the United States Post Office who admitted he was paid thirty-seven thousand dollars a year to do nothing. A labor and employee relations expert, the official had once handled contracts between the union employees and the postal service, but then he was given a supposedly lateral transfer. From that point on he did little but visit and read during his eight-to-five workday. Needless to say, he was dissatisfied with his job.

When a job is too easy or not sufficiently challenging for a person's abilities, a condition known as stress underload develops.

Psychologist Marianne Frankenhaeuser, of the University of Stockholm, studied the relationship of job satisfaction and stress by measuring hormone changes of workers in different jobs.

When under stress, the body produces catecholamines (adrenaline and noradrenaline). When stress is not too severe, these hormones increase alertness and efficiency. However, overproduction of these same hormones may lead to exhaustion, ulcers, heart disease, and other health problems.

Dr. Frankenhaeuser's study found that the presence of catecholamines was highest in people with jobs that required too little work as well as in people whose jobs required too much work for their abilities. At both extremes there was a high production of these hormones and of psychosomatic complaints. However, absenteeism was higher for the understressed test group.

Over the years we have all become increasingly aware of the harmful effects of too much stress, but few of us stop to consider that a lack of stress hurts us as well. Too little stress is a definite type of stress in itself. Without enough stimulation the body and brain simply do not function normally.

Paradoxically, the symptoms of stress underload are similar to those of stress overload. Experiments to determine the effects of sensory deprivation on human behavior have all found that subjects report impaired judgment and reasoning ability. Many experimental subjects have found the experience of sensory deprivation to be unbearable and have asked to be released from isolation by the second day. These studies have all proved that the nervous system needs a certain amount of stimulation if it is to function effectively.

When Thule Air Base was being built by North Atlantic

constructors in Greenland, the problems created by stress underload were classic. An all-male crew of about three hundred construction people were flown in to begin the project. The location of the base was about seven hundred miles from the North Pole and the climate was unusually unfriendly. Darkness was so intense that the men had trouble finding their way around once they got outside lighted areas, and temperatures were as low as forty-two degrees Fahrenheit.

Conditions were even worse on the icecap where most activity took place. There, temperatures averaged minus sixty Fahrenheit, and winds often got up to a hundred and twenty-five knots. When winds exceeded sixty knots men were confined to quarters for as many as three days.

When the construction crew was working, the pattern of their days included about ten hours of work, three hours for meals, and eight hours for sleep. That totaled only twenty-one hours, and they were faced with three more hours in which to do something.

Dr. Rupert Burtan was medical director for the project and witnessed at first hand the effects of sensory deprivation on the men. "There were some people who began to hallucinate because of the lack of stimulation in their environment," he says. "We literally had to put them in strait jackets."

Other men in the isolated camp got very violent. "One man put his fist through a wall," Dr. Burtan says. "He just went completely out of control."

Some men simply went into a catatonic state, and others developed alcohol problems even though regulations did not permit alcohol on the base.

When conditions changed and twenty-four hours of daylight became the norm, there was a new set of problems. Even though crew members had been chosen carefully and selectively for their ability to handle arctic conditions, some men could not sleep. This was in spite of the fact that lightproof blinds were standard features in all the rooms. Exhaustion brought with it its own unique set of stresses.

Dr. Burtan's medical cases were most often those in which sensory deprivation was initially responsible. In this situation, the stress underload caused by monotony of environment, isolation from people, and lack of outside stimulation created problems which impacted the performance of all workers.

The University of Michigan's Research Center for Group Dynamics interviewed two thousand men from twenty-three occupations to determine the effects of workload on job satisfaction. The occupations of their subjects ranged from factory workers to school administrators.

In their survey, the Research Center found that family doctors worked the longest hours (more than fifty-five each week) and had the heaviest workloads; their work demanded a high level of concentration. In spite of this, they reported high job satisfaction and comparatively little depression or anxiety. There were few incidences of insomnia, irritability, poor appetite, or similar stress-related problems.

In contrast, assembly-line workers complained of job dissatisfaction, depression, poor appetite, insomnia, and other physical problems. However, their jobs were typified by little responsibility, normal hours, and a regular pace.

The high-pressure jobs with long hours are generally not

the ones that cause the most stress. It is the job with stress underload attributable to monotonous, unchallenging work that is inherently more stressful.

Depression, indigestion, alcoholism, overeating, tension, and fatigue have often been directly traced to stress underload. While no conclusive nationwide survey on the subject has ever been conducted, it is clear that a major portion of the population suffers from this problem at one time or another.

While stress underload is a problem for a significant number of workers, the opposite problem of too much stress affects a greater number of working people. Ted is a manager who really produces. Anyone walking into his office sees a man who is keyed up, alert, decisive, and moving purposefully. On one winter Monday his agenda listed a sixty-page report due the following week, an interim update due that afternoon on an important account, and preparations for a four-day trip he was leaving on the following morning.

After lunch he found on his desk a memo from his boss. It requested a complete set of figures on a new account and asked that they be ready for a brief meeting the following morning. With an already impossible workload facing him, this request left Ted feeling completely overwhelmed. By midafternoon he had a splitting headache, and when he went to bed that night he was totally exhausted and still couldn't get to sleep.

The harder Ted worked that week, the less he seemed to accomplish. He was nervous and tense. A generally easygoing person, he became overly sensitive and hostile. His resulting loss of objectivity made him difficult to deal with.

He knew he wasn't coping well with the pressure he was under. He became indecisive and confused with simple problems, and his capacity for productive work was severely reduced.

Clearly, Ted was a victim of stress overload. Unrealistic deadline demands and inflexible behavior on the part of a boss who was too demanding were factors that pushed him beyond his stress capacity. The signs were easy to read: reduced performance, lowered confidence, loss of objectivity, defensiveness, irritability, poor judgment, mental confusion, strained interpersonal relations, fatigue, and insomnia.

It is important to remember that Ted was under a fair amount of stress even before he received his boss's memo. The difference was that before then, tight as things were, he felt he could handle everything that needed to be done. He was tensely energized, the kind of tension an archer uses to speed his arrow: purposeful and calculated. The memo literally changed the effects of the tension, like a little extra tug that breaks a bowstring.

This example raises questions which have significant implications for organizational policies. It directs attention to policies regarding the amount of stress experienced by employees in everyday organizational life. Management can use this information to their advantage by increasing the amount of stress where it can improve job performance and reducing stress when it becomes non-productive.

Such a policy was dramatically illustrated when General Motors increased overtime during peak seasons of the year. By the time employees had worked their seventh or eighth weekend, production dropped off, mistakes accelerated, and on-the-job injuries increased. People were so emotionally and physically fatigued by then that it was actually costing General Motors money to work them overtime; production was little better than during weeks with no overtime, and expenses were greater.

Westinghouse conducted a study years ago which illustrated that, when work environments are relaxed, productivity increases. It was found that painting the walls a pleasant color, arranging for maximum lighting, playing background music, and putting in break times did increase production up to a certain point.

In the light of the Westinghouse study and other similar reports, it may be to the advantage of many corporations to take a closer look at the work environment and pressure placed on workers. This will help them determine whether productivity and job performance are being increased or decreased by current practices.

The information poses a challenge to current management policies. A supervisor's manner of meeting his responsibilities greatly affects the stress and performance of his subordinates. Even under the same working conditions, some employees may experience more stress than others.

Some ways in which employers can decrease on-the-job stress overload for their employees are offered by Dr. Bruce Meglino of the University of South Carolina's College of Business Administration:

1. Adjust the standards for quantity or allow more time so the job seems easier.

2. Reduce the job to its essential elements and decrease the number of decisions an employee has to make.

3. Offer help in a non-evaluative manner by waiting until formal review sessions to evaluate outcomes of performance.

4. Clarify performance standards to reduce uncertainty of success.

If an employer's problem is that a job assignment is too easy for a given employee who is capable of superior performance, Dr. Meglino suggests the following:

1. Adjust standards to make the job moderately difficult.

2. Increase the number of performance evaluations.

3. Give the employee more job responsibility and involvement in decision-making.

4. Set more deadlines.

Stress can exert both a positive and a negative influence, so the task of management is to evaluate the level of job difficulty in relation to an individual worker's capacity for handling stress. Real management skill involves adjusting the level of job stress to the point where an employee can produce a peak performance.

Recognizing the Clues to Stress Underload and Overload

In determining the level of stress for superior job performance, it is necessary to recognize the clues to stress underload and overload. The following survey can help you identify your personal stress response. Check the items which most closely describe your situation; then add your totals below.

COLUMN A

____ There is little variety or change in my work.

____ I seldom find what I am doing to be challenging or demanding.

____ I am overqualified for my current position.

____ There is a lot of time to socialize with others in my office.

____ In general, I feel bored with the work I am doing.

____ I feel apathetic and lethargic most of the time.

COLUMN B

____ I do not work well under pressure.

____ Because of my indecisiveness, I avoid making decisions.

____ Little things make me irritable.

____ I have trouble sleeping at night.

____ People find me impatient to get things done.

____ I am tense and anxious most of the time.

____ I usually take work home with me.

_____ Unless I push my-
self, I am rarely mo-
tivated to get things
done.

_____ My job requires little responsibility or
initiative.

_____ Basically, I work a
nine-to-five job.

_____ I seldom look for-
ward to going to
work.

_____ I feel tired and depressed for no ap-
parent reason.

_____ I have been making
more mistakes than
usual.

===== TOTAL   ===== TOTAL

If you have six or more checks in either column, you
have a stress problem. Six or more checks in Column A is
indicative of stress underload; six or more checks in Column B show you are suffering from stress overload. If you
have checked five or more statements in each column, you
may have a stress problem in different areas of your life at
the same time.

Tips to Reduce Stress Underload and Stress Overload

Stress underload and overload in a job situation may not
always call for a remedy as drastic as a job change. If you

are suffering from one or the other, try any or all of the tips listed:

1. If you are bored with your job, change your routine or do something innovative such as trying a new restaurant for lunch.

2. See what new positions may be opening up in your company. Check what skills those positions require, and see whether or not you qualify for any of those jobs.

3. Take a challenging evening course or work toward a degree which may give you better job opportunities.

4. Write a list of things you would like to accomplish each day. Then set out to do them.

5. Seek to accomplish one task at a time whether at work or at home. Do the most important task first.

6. Get involved in a competitive sport or start doing regular physical exercise.

7. Equalize your pressures by balancing difficult tasks with less demanding ones. If you can't do this, take frequent breaks.

8. When pressures begin to mount, take a coffee break or walk around the building.

9. Stop rushing; pace yourself better. Needless hurrying burns up energy.

10. The next time something irritates you, ask yourself, "Is this worth getting upset over?"

Your Five Levels of Coping with Stress

Every individual seems to have a different level of effectiveness for coping with stress. Actually, these may be determined by the style of coping they use. Styles may vary from a go-for-it eagerness to a reluctance that translates into an inability to work.

The five levels of stress style presented here are meant to be a means of evaluating yourself in different stressful situations. An honest appraisal will probably show that you, like most other people, react at different levels in different situations. That awareness can be your key to improving the over-all way in which you handle stressful circumstances.

LEVEL 1: "THIS COULD PUT US IN THE BIG TIME!"

The true achiever blooms when the demands are greatest. His outlook is so positive, he sometimes has difficulty characterizing the pressure as stress because the word sounds so negative to him. Where another person would perceive taxing demands, he perceives opportunity. From past experience and present observation, he can sense that stressful situations, while intimidating others, actually create an advantage for him. His instinctive response to pressure is to mobilize all his emotional and creative forces toward tackling the problems at hand.

Physically and intellectually, the achiever is at his peak when coping with an unusually stressful challenge. He can work long hours without fatigue. By keeping sight of the ultimate goal, he will usually develop a game plan to take full advantage of the time on hand so he can maximize his opportunity.

The achiever will feel a slight letdown upon completion of his project, regardless of success or failure.

Others may find this person to be unnaturally energetic, but he is a true leader.

LEVEL 2: "I'M CERTAIN WE CAN HANDLE IT."

The person who has this response to a stress situation is likely to experience, however briefly, a feeling of both excitement and dread when facing the actual stress circumstance. After taking an overview of the problem, however, he can rough out strategies and perform very capably.

He is never as eager under stress as a Level 1 person because he makes an effort to keep both risks and opportunities in mind at all times. He tries to be realistic and continually re-evaluates the situation to ensure that he is alert and prepared for any eventuality.

The harder he works, the calmer and more capable the Level 2 person becomes. This is not to say he does not sometimes feel keyed up physically and emotionally.

The difference between the Level 1 achiever and the Level 2 performer is that the latter's sense of well-being under pressure comes from *handling* a situation. In contrast, the Level 1 person's satisfaction comes from *exploiting* the stress situation.

A Level 2 individual will do a good job with details if he is confident someone else is overseeing the project. He can be typically characterized as well prepared.

LEVEL 3: "TELL ME WHAT TO DO AND I CAN GO ALONG WITH IT."

The person who feels this way when confronted with a stress opportunity will put up cheerfully with a pressure situation. He will manage limited responsibility quite competently.

Emotionally, he tries to minimize the feeling of stress, and therefore he will tend to act as if everything were business as usual. He may be compulsive about routines when presented with new strategies for coping with situations that arise. For example, he will probably put out extra effort to finish a task by the end of the day. In this way he can achieve temporary periods in which business really is as usual, and consequently he will appear to be very steady.

With guidance, the Level 3 individual will go steadily from one phase to the next. However, he would rather not be bothered with having to think about the whole scheme of a project.

Although he is personally not as motivated as a Level 1 or Level 2 person, he can get into the spirit of a demanding project. He is very relieved, though, when it is all over.

LEVEL 4: "IF IT MUST BE, IT MUST BE . . . AS LONG AS IT DOESN'T LAST TOO LONG!"

When operating under stress, the Level 4 person will be less productive and less alert than he would be under routine conditions. The stress will make him feel tense and more easily irritated. Disruptions of a task will unhinge him.

Like the Level 3 individual, he does not want the responsibility of taking the overview; he prefers to do and think of only one task at a time. Unlike a Level 3 person, however, he is always hopeful that each task is the final step of a project.

LEVEL 5:   "YIKES! I'D LIKE TO GET OUT OF HERE!!"

Stress definitely has a detrimental effect on this person. It brings on fatigue, depression, and nervousness. Initially resentful of the extra workload, the Level 5 person will be more likely to make mistakes, and this will only aggravate the pressure he perceives.

He needs handholding. Even if others get into the spirit, he will resist the momentum. He may be mentally absent, or he may go so far as to not go to work at all.

From the beginning, the attitude of a Level 5 person will be visibly one of hoping the whole situation will terminate soon. He is not likely to pull his share when in a pressured environment, and he can have a measurably bad effect on the morale of those around him.

No person will perform at any one level all the time. Ideally, we would like to function at Levels 1 or 2, but this is not always possible or probable.

Often, stress may push us a bit beyond our threshold. We will then be likely to react with a Level 3 approach: we can still function on the job, but we do experience a strain. As the stress becomes more severe and prolonged, our behavior may begin to produce a Level 4 or 5 reaction. When we reach that level we will experience a performance breakdown.

These five levels should help you recognize situations in which you are working within your optimal stress level. They will also help you identify the signals of stress overload.

How Modern Man Reacts to Stress

It is 7:05 A.M., an hour later than the time the alarm was set to go off. This is the morning Jerry is to leave town on an important business trip. When he wakes up he looks at the clock and frantically jumps out of bed. If he hurries, he will still have time to catch his plane.

Twenty-seven minutes later he carries his luggage to the car. He is out of breath but ready to go. As he fumbles in his pockets for the car keys he gets a sinking feeling. They're not there. Suddenly he remembers he let his son borrow the car the night before. After a quick sprint to retrieve the keys, he is finally ready to go.

Traffic is slower than usual because of rush-hour traffic. When Jerry finally gets to the airport his muscles are tight and his heart is racing. But there are more delays. The line is long at the ticket counter, and by the time he pays for his flight he has only five minutes left until departure time. That time is quickly used up at the airport security booth where a long line of conventioneers precedes him.

Jerry arrives at his terminal gate just in time to see his

plane taxi down the runway. Helpless to do anything about the situation, his stomach is tied up in knots and his pulse is pounding. Emotionally, he is drained. His body, activated by a stress mechanism, is in a state of complete alarm.

In threatening or frustrating situations, the body goes through a number of chemical and hormonal changes. These responses are as old as man himself and were actually responsible for the survival of the human species.

When primitive man stepped out of his cave he took a quick but thorough look around for predators. Like all other animals, he ventured only as far as safety permitted. If by chance he was waylaid by a mastodon while en route to a sheltering cave, he needed to react immediately. In that situation his body would automatically prepare him to do one of two things: fight physically or flee from the danger.

It was stress that provided primitive man with the extra strength and co-ordination necessary to overcome or escape a big cat or other carnivore. When faced with a threat, the hypothalamus activates the pituitary gland. This gland then releases a chemical called ACTH. An immediate chain reaction is then set off within the endocrine system.   .

Prehistoric man's blood flashed adrenal secretions that gave him strength in the form of sugar and stored fats. This strength communicated to his muscles and to his brain. Instantly, full energy was mobilized and stimulated his pulse, respiration, and blood pressure. His digestive processes turned off at once, insuring that no energy would be diverted from meeting the threat. His coagulation chemistry prepared to resist wounds from fang and claw with quick clotting. Senses were sharpened. Red blood cells poured from the spleen into the accelerated blood circulation so the respiratory system could gulp more oxygen.

Harvard physiologist Dr. Walter B. Cannon termed this reaction the "fight or flight response" as a way of describing the body's adaptation to a variety of life-threatening situations. The entire physical and mental system, when reacting this way, is geared to protect the body from any harm.

Modern man still reacts in much the same way as his Stone Age ancestor did. Although today's threats are more likely to be mental or emotional, the physiological strain is still there.

The stream of upsets and delays, the frantic rushing and frustration Jerry went through in trying to reach his plane, all contributed to putting this same response into motion. And any of his modern peers would have reacted similarly under the same circumstances.

A variety of contemporary situations could induce the fight or flight response. A long-term assistant vice-president, when handed a press release announcing company promotions that does not include his name, would be likely to react with this response. A competent sales manager told she was due for relocation might also react this way. Like the threat of physical attack, these situations produce stress.

For early man, stress was a life saver. It produced a physiological reaction that enabled him to produce extra reservoirs of energy for fending off a stalking predator.

Modern man, unable to hurl even a ballpoint pen at a mail clerk, must suppress these same physiological reactions. His ability to do so is interpreted as confidence and control, qualities of paramount importance in maintaining leadership over others. Thus, the surge of adrenalin, increased heartbeat, and muscle readiness are of virtually no use to him in fighting off life threats.

Modern man has no place to direct stress-induced reactions. He therefore usually directs them on himself. They then quite literally eat him. If this continues over a sustained period of time, the body's defensive reactions wear down and eventually give place to fatigue, exhaustion, and illness.

Ironically, the same responses which saved primitive man are killing modern man. Prolonged stress has been blamed for ulcers, hypertension, heart attacks, tension, and migraine headaches. Even insomnia, alcoholism, and drug abuse can be tied directly to stress overload.

Release Those Bottled-up Feelings

In Japan many major companies like Panasonic have a "Time Out Room" where workers can go to relieve frustration and pent-up anger. It is soundproof and padded and contains a large stuffed dummy. Employees are encouraged to go to this room if someone or something irritates them during the day. There they can punch, scream, kick, or tell off the dummy with no repercussions.

Does this sound odd? It shouldn't. Studies have shown that, after releasing stored anger, a person's tension level and blood pressure are greatly reduced, as well as accidents on the job. Since it is unlikely that your company has a Time Out Room, you may need to rely on other methods of releasing built-up tensions. And it is important that they be released; the only other alternative is to let them vent their damage on you.

Effective ways of releasing your physiological stress responses are:

1. Keep a tennis ball in your desk and squeeze or pound it the next time someone irritates you.

2. Buy a large beanbag and punch away at it whenever frustrated. Imagine it to be the person who may have caused your anger.

3. Keep a dart board and a picture of the person most responsible for your stress (such as your boss). The next time he bothers you, attach the picture to your dart board and fire away.

4. Get out into an open space and let out some primal screams or four-letter words. Or do this while driving on the freeway.

If these suggestions seem too extreme for you, there are more conventional ways in which you can unload bad feelings.

1. Run or jog in place for at least five minutes while thinking of something pleasant.

2. Climb a flight of stairs two steps at a time.

3. Take a quick walk around the building and do some deep breathing.

4. Play a fierce, competitive game of handball, racquetball, or tennis.

5. Hold a telephone book in each hand and lift them like weights.

Coping with Stress

Stress is a fact of life. It expresses itself in physical, mental, and emotional forms and must be dealt with accordingly.

While stress is inevitable, it is not necessarily negative. Working at the optimal stress level will produce peak productivity. Stress becomes negative only when it exists in insufficient or, more commonly, excessive amounts.

The key to arriving at optimal stress level lies first in determining what that level is for each individual. Then techniques for decreasing or increasing stress may be used to create a working environment and job description that allow for superior productivity.

ORGANIZATIONAL STRESS

How Organizations Unwittingly Create Stress

Like individuals, corporations have distinctive personalities. They also have different styles and outlooks, just as style and outlook may vary from one family to the next.

The tone of an organization is set largely by its top executives. However, it is also influenced by organizational structure and the type of people drawn to that structure.

While the style and approach of an organization are determined by its structure and its people, their effectiveness will be determined largely by the organization's climate. This is partly due to the negative or positive impressions people feel as a result of that climate.

The climate of an organization is the environment in which it operates or conducts business. The climate is determined not only by the physical environment but by the emotional environment, which reflects employee attitudes, ways of operating, and manners of interaction.

Organizations are set up to evaluate tangibles, so the intangible nature of company climate often bars it from automatic analysis. Therefore, some designated element in the organization needs to keep a finger on the pulse of said climate. Since the top executive plays an important part in the evolution of the climate, he is usually the ideal person to be on the lookout for any changes in it.

Several years ago, *Dun's Review* carried an article which listed the ten most stressful companies in America from an employee's point of view. The report was based on input from executive recruiters and management consultants. Companies included in the list were Revlon, ITT, Chrysler, Singer, Gallo Winery, Wachovia, Procter & Gamble, Johnson & Johnson, Crane, and W. R. Grace & Co.

In most of these companies, the factor which determined the amount of stress employees experienced was the personality of the chief executive. A tyrannical executive generally had subordinates who operated in fear. However, if a chief executive was too weak his employees were constantly under the pressure of factional struggles.

The stress at Revlon was caused partly by the highly competitive nature of the industry. More influential than that, however, were the extraordinary demands made on the staff by founder Charles Revson.

ITT stress was traced to fear. At the time of the survey, Chairman Harold Geneen's decision to fire one hundred executives started rumors of other large-scale firings. This in turn created a wave of dismissals which left most employees afraid for their jobs.

Other companies on the *Dun's Review* list were there for different reasons. Following enormous company losses, Chrysler was taken over by new management, which naturally caused staff and procedural changes. The tense atmosphere at Gallo Winery was directly traced to its hard-driving chief executive, Ernest Gallo. He insisted on superior performance and would quickly discharge any executive who did not measure up to his standards.

The personality of the chief executive can seriously disrupt the smooth flow of a large organization's operation. If he is too stubborn, his insistence on having his own way will stifle creativity and inhibit initiative.

Flint Whitlock was the former public relations director for a professional soccer team. He blames the personality of the general manager as the reason he left that position. "My boss appeared easygoing to the public, but those who worked with him found the inconsistency in his behavior confusing to deal with," he says. "His rules were capricious, and he would consistently make irrational threats concerning employment so that the work climate was always laden with fear. You just can't get productive work in an environment like that."

Van Spurgeon, vice-president of Wetterau Industry, believes the chief executive creates a great deal of stress if members of his organization feel only he can make decisions. "If anyone calls his hand or implies projects have not been moving sufficiently quickly, they risk losing their jobs.

"Most people don't realize how the organizational climate affects the stress level of all employees," Spurgeon says. "At Wetterau we completed a study of twenty divisions and pinpointed four where stress was beyond healthy limits. It is amazing that in three of the four divisions we would never have guessed by the outward appearances that there was so much stress."

Once stress overload was determined to have risen to

unhealthy levels in some divisions, Wetterau could begin the process of eliminating the pressure source and thus increase productivity.

Fierce competition generated at executive levels can be debilitating to an entire organizational force. If the motivation for competition is that of qualifying a successor to the chief executive, that very competition may make the individual a threat to the executive who started the competition in the first place. The natural result is that the threatened executive will fire the most competent individual, the one who presents the greatest threat to him, and in that way he will eventually eliminate his best employees.

Any major changes among top executives can also cause harmful stress overload. Promotions have reverberations throughout an organization and, when handled improperly, may even affect friendships. If the friendship of two individuals who have to rely on each other or answer to one another is affected, organizational productivity will be seriously hampered. If promotions are delayed for too long, competitors may develop antipathies which will later alter their willingness to operate as a team.

Delays of promotions will affect more than just the executives involved. They will also cause rumors down to the lowest employment level. Throughout the whole organization uncertainty will cause stress overload as employees talk about real or imagined changes to their jobs that would be effected by the individual they think will be promoted. This will also cloud their perception of the new supervisor or executive when he is finally promoted.

When promotions are imminent, one of employees' greatest fears is that their new superior will be a person with an abrasive personality. Such an individual generally criticizes frequently and undiplomatically. He often is quick to point out the errors in the plans of others thus effectively squelching their motivation for creativity.

The executive with an autocratic personality generally has a superior skill for analysis, but his inability to delegate makes him something less than effective as a leader. However, he usually assumes that his subordinates and co-workers will accept his decisions and logic simply because they are his, and he will become enraged if this expectation is not met.

The total control and rigidity with which the autocratic personality runs a company makes him unable to compromise; compromise strikes him as defecting for lower standards. Consequently he does not possess the flexibility necessary for the give-and-take of organizational growth.

If an executive's personality does not inspire trust in his subordinates, employee morale and hence company productivity can be seriously impaired. Mistrust can lead to job dissatisfaction, poor communication, and ultimately to bad decision-making because the executive will not have the necessary information on which to base good decisions; his perception of reality will be impaired.

It is unfortunate that those in high-level positions can use their power inappropriately to create a stressful working environment. Power actually denotes their ability to acquire and use whatever is needed to achieve their work goals. Since it involves having access to whatever is needed to get the job done, it can be abused into a means for domination and control of other people.

The most effective leaders do have definite power, which

they often use, but they also have credibility. This means they are listened to, but they also listen and hence will be personally interested in a subordinate's growth.

Power struggles within an organization are another source of severe stress. A by-product of those struggles—heightened competition—increases the pressure even more.

Some companies unwittingly create the stress inherent to power struggles by making it necessary for employees to have political alliances if they are to get ahead. Alliances in themselves are not harmful; if among peers, alliances can advance a group as a whole. It is the political alliance that is detrimental, for it does not always direct its power upward.

Political alliances often focus their concentration on making their alliance look better than another. The technique they use to do this is frequently to damage the other alliance's work or make it look less effective, and this in turn damages the effectiveness of the entire organization.

The political alliance is also damaging because it uses valuable production time to campaign for and acquire allies. Since the campaigner is often the person at the top of the political alliance, and also within company management levels, the work time used is generally that of one of the most valuable organization employees.

Executives caught up in power games and political alliances generate enormous pressures on their subordinates. If excessive, these pressures can virtually destroy the organization. At the least, they will weaken loyalty and cause a breakdown of discipline.

An important factor in the stress climate of an organization is the type of individual a chief executive hires to manage his corporation.

Some people are attracted to a particular organization because they think they would feel comfortable with its approach to success; it appeals to their personalities. Other people are selectively chosen for the impact their personalities will have on the company. Both processes of employee absorption can be attributed directly to the chief executive; he sets the climate that attracts some personalities, and he takes the initiative responsible for the hiring of others.

It is often the mismatch between the personality of the employee and the personality, or climate, of the organization which creates stressful circumstances. An individual from a strict, traditional family may get along very well with an authoritarian boss. However, he would feel extreme discomfort in a non-structured situation. In contrast, a person brought up to exercise independence and freedom of thought would feel stifled and frustrated in a work environment which was strictly structured.

Actually, for productivity to be at its highest the top executive must not only allow for the absorption of employees who blend into the company's personality; he must also manage his business as he would his family. Good parents allow their children a certain amount of independence and flexibility while simultaneously teaching them to cope with adversity and develop a strong value system.

Likewise, the good boss will create an environment that allows employees to make decisions and operate flexibly. He will want them to feel free to try innovative methods that might be more productive, and he will also want them to maintain a sense of values that will give his organization strength and enduring qualities. He is basically an instructor who helps his employees adapt by increasing their competence and providing the environment for optimal performance.

Overstressed Organizations, Like People, Break Down

Overstressed organizations, just like individuals, break down if they fail to take adaptive action whenever change poses new demands and higher requirements. If they do not immediately take measures to cope with the pressures caused by change, stress overload will be the inevitable result.

Organizational stress overload which is sufficiently serious to result in breakdown can actually come from a variety of circumstances. The first and most obvious would be the accumulated stress overload or underload of each individual employee. Employees suffering from too much tension or not enough stimulation will not operate at anything close to optimal productivity. If this spreads throughout the plant, fear caused by inability to meet goals and demands will produce either apathy or panic. Either reaction will inhibit the group from dealing constructively with any crises or problems, and the organization's breakdown is thus virtually insured.

Lack of group esteem can lead to a similar breakdown. This deficiency can be caused by anything from a boss whose demands are so unreasonable that they practically guarantee failure to a structure that demands so little of employees they feel they have little to be proud of. However, the result of this lack will be equivalent to that of sensory deprivation; employees will have so little confidence in their ability to succeed that they won't even attempt to do a good job. Here again, over-all company productivity will decay to the point where the business is no longer viable.

A frequent cause for the dissolution of a company which is managed by either a rigid or an autocratic personality is the loss of contact with reality. This contact is lost when lack of trust among group members, whether caused by fear of criticism or resignation to non-initiative, inhibits them from revealing their true judgments about company matters. When the top executive loses this communications source he loses his main contact with what really is happening in his company. He therefore starts making decisions with inadequate information. Since they are not decisions based upon reality they may consequently destroy his organization.

While organizations are similar to individuals in that either the stress of inadequacy or the stress of excessive demands can lead to physical breakdown, there are other ways in which they are not similar. For example, while a person can immediately relieve stress by participating in an exerting function that releases physiological tensions, organizations have no short-term cures. Their alternatives consist primarily of preplanning for any crisis. Without a game plan which shows them how they should handle an unpredictable stress situation, they may become victims of panic and panic will not allow for competent productivity.

For example, if a relocation problem within a company is an anticipated possibility rather than a remote probability, company behavior if relocation happens is likely to be constructive rather than panicky. If a group is aware of problems being confronted and has thought of how to handle them before they come up, they can identify alternatives and immediately begin to cope with stress. If they are unprepared, they will first go through a period of shock and then face accelerated restructuring. Both situations will delay the time when they can begin to act productively on the problem.

When a company preplans for possible problems, whether these problems are within the control of the company or simply results of outside events, it is important that it establish a series of priorities. These priorities will form the logic behind the solution approach adopted to cope with any crisis.

In the actual treatment of a stress overload problem, regular problem-solving procedures are essential. These should center their emphasis on decision-making and positive action, functions which are impaired when uncertainty or conflict cause organizational stress overload.

If a crisis occurs in a company and no plans have been made for coping with the ensuing stress, it will be difficult for that company to evade failure. However, it will not be impossible. While their reaction time will be severely limited, immediate and organized action can salvage the situation.

A manager's first action in coping with crisis stress may have to be something as seemingly minor as dealing with employees' hurt feelings or hostilities. Until he can apply first aid to the company family, he will be limited to making only short-term plans. However, once fear has been dealt with and casualties of the crisis have been taken care of, he can go on to making long-term plans with the same approach used for preplanning.

Whether recovering from an unexpected or an expected blow, a company must first find the source of stress and then plan for ways to eliminate that source. Allowing intensive stress to continue for a prolonged period of time will damage the organization as completely as an individual's internalized stress can damage his body.

Warning Signs of Overstressed Organizations

The following checklist is useful in determining the emotional health of your organization and detecting the danger signs of a group breakdown caused by stress overload. This material has been adapted from Dr. E. Paul Torrance's chapter "When Groups Break Down" in *Constructive Behavior: Stress, Personality and Mental Health,* Wadsworth Publishing, Inc., Belmont, CA, 1965, pp. 161–83.

If a comment describes your organization style or climate, write "yes" beside it; if it is not applicable to your situation or environment, write "no."

1. _____ Members of my organization have to be told to help one another. If someone has to be taught new job skills, or if a peer is in trouble, employees will not take the initiative to remedy the situation.

2. _____ Authority and power are in the hands of one leader.

3. _____ The leader of my organization seldom passes information down to all levels of employees. He rarely keeps one department briefed on what is happening in other departments.

4. _____ There is a lack of clear organizational goals and objectives.

5. _____ Group members do not resolve disagreements easily. In the course of airing disagreements, individuals involved have a tendency to lose their tempers and become emotional.

6. _____ My immediate group leader, or supervisor, holds tight reins of control over the work functions in my organization.

7. _____ Group members do not have sufficient information to know exactly what is expected of them.

8. _____ Individuals in my organization are unwilling to work hard to achieve predetermined goals.

9. _____ There is no sense of cohesiveness or group pride among employees.

10. _____ Decisions in my organization are generally made with unnecessary delay.

11. _____ Group members do not keep each other informed of what they are doing.

12. _____ Energies are frequently dissipated through interpersonal bickering or through the pursuit of personal ambitions.

13. _____ Accidents are frequent.

14. _____ Coercion is used to get individuals to carry out requests and decisions.

15. _____ There is an overemphasis on conformity in my organization. Blocks to independent thinking are frequently used.

16. _____ Group members are concerned only with meeting requirements. They easily lose sight of the main goals.

17. _____ Joking around my organization is generally vicious and tends to exclude certain members of the group.

18. _____ The leader of my organization does not back up those to whom he delegates authority.

19. _____ Disagreements and differences of opinions between employees and executives are not permitted in my organization.

20. _____ Short cuts are used to get out of work or training.

_____ TOTAL

The number of statements you agreed with on the preceding checklist determines the degree of organizational breakdown within your company. If you checked between sixteen and twenty statements, your organization is in danger of not functioning. Eleven to fifteen statements designated in your tally of responses indicates an impending breakdown. If you agreed with six to ten of the statements, your organization is experiencing a good emotional climate, and a very healthy organizational climate is indicated if you checked five or fewer statements.

The preceding checklist can also be useful in determining the source of your organizational problems.

Organizations cannot be held together unless they have a positive degree of member compatibility, power, communication among members, and clearly defined objectives and goals.

If you checked statement 1, 5, 9, 13, or 17 on the checklist, the source of your organizational stress may be traced to unhealthy interpersonal relationships. The cure for your organizational stress overload is therefore an attempt to establish more harmonious interpersonal relationships among your employees.

If you checked statement 2, 6, 10, 14, or 18, the cause of organizational breakdown in your company may come from an unhealthy distribution of power.

If your checklist shows a "yes" beside statement 3, 7, 11, 15, or 19, you may need to look to the health of your organization's communication system when seeking to minimize stress overload.

And if you checked statement 4, 8, 12, 16, or 20, there is a problem with the structure and development of common organizational objectives and goals.

Clearly, if any of the four aspects is weak, each of the others is likely to weaken. Therefore, if you have checked statements in one category, it is likely that you also checked statements in another of the four categories.

While weakness in any one of the four areas signals the need to minimize tension immediately, a group or company may still function with limited effectiveness if the other three areas are healthy.

The Skyrocketing Cost of Stress

The mental and physical effects of job stress have long been recognized as a disruptive influence on the individual. However, evidence is now beginning to point to the impact this same stress has on the economy.

One contemporary estimate indicates that, for executives alone, American industry loses between ten and twenty billion dollars annually through lost workdays, hospitalization, and early death caused by stress.

Heart disease accounts for more than half the deaths in the United States. It also is responsible for an annual loss of 132 million workdays.

In an attempt to reduce health costs and sick leave, the United Storeworkers' Union at Gimbels in New York City organized an experimental program with Cornell University Medical College. The purpose of the program was to detect and treat hypertension on the job.

At the beginning of the program, 1,859 Gimbels employees were screened for high blood pressure. Of the 186 determined to have high blood pressure, two thirds accepted free treatment for the next year. This treatment included medication and checkups by nurses and paraprofessionals. The union took an active part in the program by sending reminders and telephoning individuals who missed their appointments.

A year after the program began, tests showed the 81 per cent of the workers treated for hypertension had a satisfactory reduction in blood pressure. Most individuals reduced their blood pressure levels within just three months and experienced only minimal side effects.

Since the union volunteered much of the administrative work and a sympathetic manufacturer donated the drugs, the complete cost of treating each Gimbels hypertensive employee was less than a hundred dollars per patient.

The key to the success of the United Storeworkers' Union program was that it was organized and implemented in the work environment. Patients had no direct costs and lost no work time, and medical efficiency was increased by using paraprofessionals.

In the long run, programs like this reap a cost savings by reducing a major risk factor in coronaries. Unfortunately, most companies are not so dollar wise. Many organizations spend millions of dollars annually to reduce industrial accidents. However, for every employee who dies from industrial hazards or accidents, fifty employees die from cardiovascular diseases. And cardiovascular diseases definitely are often caused by stress-related disorders.

At least 85 per cent of all work accidents are caused by the inability to cope with emotional stress. An obvious way in which this happens is that, while distracted by concentrating on an emotionally stressful problem, employees are not as careful to avoid accidents. A less obvious way is that employees try to escape their work through alcohol, which then causes a reduction in all their perception senses.

It is estimated that twelve million Americans are alcoholics. Not included in this figure are the untold numbers of "closet alcoholics" who hide their problem. Statistics from dozens of major corporations show that one out of every ten employees has an alcohol problem. The National Institute on Alcohol Abuse and Alcoholism recently revealed that this problem alone costs American industry almost sixteen billion dollars a year in absenteeism and medical costs.

The average alcoholic is a man or woman in the mid-thirties who has a good job, a good home, and a family. The problem is most common among middle managers and technically skilled workers, and those who do suffer from it generally waste at least one fourth of their production time on the job.

Problem drinkers quite simply make costly employees. Since they not only waste time while on the job but also miss some days altogether and tend to have high health and accident problems, some estimates show they cost at least twice as much as other employees.

Many companies are beginning to adopt a new policy toward alcoholism. They see it as a treatable disease rather than a condition for disciplinary action. In fact, confirmed alcoholics in a number of corporations qualify for major medical benefits if they will accept specific treatment.

The attitude that alcoholism is a treatable disease has saved some companies a substantial amount of money. The Oldsmobile Division of General Motors Corporation in Lansing, Michigan, recently spent $57,000 in treatment and hospitalization costs to put 117 employees through its voluntary Employee Alcoholism Recovery Program. The first twenty-five employees who completed the program cut their wage-waste (wages lost due to high absenteeism) from $85,000 to $45,000, and this figure did not include the company's savings both in greater production and in money paid to replacement employees.

Alcoholism, a stress-related problem, costs a great deal of money, but psychosomatic diseases also account for a major portion of industry's stress tab. While psychosomatic problems induced by stress create high rates of absenteeism, they also affect industry costs by causing high turnover rates in employment. Replacement costs for employees may be as high as six weeks' salary when lost production time is averaged in along with double salaries. Every executive or employee lost through early retirement, death, disability, or relocation means the company forfeits whatever man-hours it took to train him, but it also loses the intangible values of relationships he built up and contacts he cultivated outside the firm.

When a forty-five-year-old employee dies, the loss is enormous. It constitutes the accumulated production he could have contributed to his company between ages forty-five and retirement at sixty-five or older.

Psychiatrists and physicians who have worked in business report that about 80 per cent of all employee emotional problems are stress related. They agree that as many as half of all dismissals and resignations are also due to emotional, or stress, difficulties and not to technical inadequacies.

To deal with the economic factor that mental health is,

many businesses are developing positive programs. Mental health has been described as the ability to cope with the demands of one's environment, so the main focus of mental health programs is to help individuals cope with whatever stress they encounter in their day-to-day activities.

The fact that many employees have difficulty coping with stress can easily be verified. Five hundred and twenty-five thousand Americans use tranquilizers, consuming $200 million worth of them annually.

The most popular tranquilizers, Valium and Librium, act on the central nervous system. They reduce mental alertness and can reduce motor performance to the extent that it results in job errors and accidents. They may provide temporary relief from stress, but they also prevent a person from learning the coping skills necessary to deal with stress.

Headaches are another manifestation of stress. They affect nearly a quarter of the American population each year and are the leading cause of lost time in business and industry.

Another stress-induced illness is ulcers. It has been estimated that 10 per cent of the nation's population will suffer from them at some time in their lives.

When a person suffers from a stress-induced illness, his company's expenses do not revolve around just his lack of performance. Expenses also add up for the work of others, which is slowed down or otherwise affected by the sick person's inability to do his job adequately.

Bob is a good example of this. A sales manager in a large city, he did an outstanding job his first two years on the job. Then he began to lose some of his best salesmen and productivity dropped. Distressed, Bob stopped showing up for work regularly.

Fortunately, he decided to go in for a physical about this time. That led to an appointment with the company's consulting psychiatrist. When Bob decided to go into psychoanalysis, it was found that he had two conflicting obsessions: he had an inordinate ambition, and he also had a crippling fear of the consequences of success. That conflict created unbearable tension and depression, which then communicated itself to the employees around him.

The solution for Bob was to stay out of management and stick to sales. There he was successful and served his company well, but the pressure for performance was less.

How an individual will handle stress is determined not only by the pressures his company allows to build up on the job but also by his very personality. It is the goodness of fit between the demands of the job and the abilities of the person, between the needs of the person and the degree to which the needs are satisfied in the job environment, which will determine the amount of strain.

The person who handles stress well often has several obvious characteristics. He is generally flexible, active, and productive, but he also accepts his own capacities and limitations. His source of gratification is not centered in just one area of his life, and he treats others as individuals.

Therefore, the company that wants to encourage stress-coping abilities in its employees will encourage the use of these same characteristics. It will set an example in treating its employees as individuals so they in turn will treat each other that way. It will be flexible in its policies, but not so flexible that rules and expectations lose their definition.

And while a certain amount of conformity is necessary in any group, it will allow for and create a climate in which creativity and independence will be encouraged.

Reducing Organizational Stress

It is true that modern organizations have an impact on both the psychological and the physiological health of their members. While it is also true that the most visible form of this stress is negative, there are several innovative measures available to management for containing stress at productive levels.

1. STRESS ALTERATION may be the first technique some companies need to use when looking for ways to avoid employee health problems. The amount of stress is not the problem in this situation; it is the source of stress that makes it damaging.

    If employee job stresses stem from role ambiguity or conflict, or if they are the result of poor interpersonal relationships with fellow workers, they will be bad for both the health of the employee and that of the organization. The answer here is not to institute a series of formal job descriptions; that action would eliminate necessary flexibility. Rather, adoption of a practice involving frequent discussions between each man and his supervisor for the purpose of redefining his job responsibilities is often successful. This lets the employee know what is expected of him but also allows for alterations in the job description whenever the situation calls for it. Job stress will then be the positive pressure of having to meet demands, rather than the negative pressure of uncertainty.

2. ENVIRONMENT ALTERATION is the logical solution to a situation in which stress overload is being caused by excessive demands. Increasing an employee's resources for reducing overload and deadline pressure, even if this means obtaining auxiliary help, may actually effect a savings for the company. In large corporations, the elimination of many of the hierarchical levels of the organization will increase communication between personnel and decrease duplication of work. When environment alteration is effected, however, it is necessary to verify that all employees know how to use their new resources.

3. USE OF PARTICIPATION is frequently an effective antidote to stress resulting from job dissatisfaction and job-related threats. An essential element when employees are encouraged to participate in a wider variety of projects, however, is supervisory support. Otherwise, employees will feel as though they are being tested, and the objective of increasing their confidence will not be met.

When a company institutes a participation policy, it is important that it be prepared to ask for relevant participation. Illusory participation, such as a supervisor who asks for the opinion of a subordinate and then ignores it, will have no effect on the stress problem. Trivial participation which allows an employee to be involved in seemingly insignificant decisions will possibly aggravate the problem; the employee will feel demeaned if he is allowed to make only minor decisions.

The only type of participation that will make employees feel more a part of their organization is that which is relevant and legitimate. The employees must feel that any decisions delegated to them are legitimately theirs to make. They must also feel those decisions will have an impact on company operations.

4. TRAINING is an obvious solution to some types of organizational stress. This will reduce the amount of effort an employee has to expend in completing certain assignments; confidence in his ability and complete knowledge of how to accomplish the task at hand will make that task seem less difficult than it would have been without specific training.

5. SELECTIVITY in placement of employees will eliminate some organizational stress before it happens. This selectivity should take note not only of skill qualifications but also of tolerance for ambiguity, ability to handle role conflict, resistance to the stress of responsibility, or any other environmental factors that might affect performance of a job.

6. TERM LIMITATIONS may be an alternative to be considered in a few rare situations. Jobs which are typified by unusually severe stress should sometimes be put on a rotation basis if they cannot be restructured. The presidency of the United States is a good example of a job with term limitations and rotation status; the person who fills that job is allowed to fill it only for a certain length of time before another individual is rotated into the position. A disadvantage of this technique, however, is that every time a new person is rotated into a position he will temporarily have to bear the additional stresses of job transfer.

These techniques are available to organizations that are actively looking after the health and productivity of their employees. They are not a cure-all; they will only remedy situations a company has the power to remedy. In addition, the individual must look out for himself.

If you are trying to cope with organizational stress overload, try some of the following suggestions.

1. Don't rely on someone else within the organization to come to your rescue. Survival within your organization is entirely up to you.

2. Do not assume that a person who makes less money than you is not a threat to you. Be prepared for the possibility that trouble might originate from anyone in the organization hierarchy, whether they are above you or below you.

3. Realize that no one is immune to competition; just because someone in the organization is close to you, likes you, and realizes your talents does not mean he is not likely to eliminate you if his advancement hinges on it.

4. Acknowledge that justice is usually sacrificed to expediency in any organization. Whenever a conflict develops between two people, the individual with the lower status will be the one who is labeled "wrong."

5. Do not let a smooth spell at work delude you into thinking everything will henceforth be "smooth sailing." Constantly guard and support your position.

6. Do not assume you can ever totally relax with anyone in the organization; confidants can quickly turn into competitors who may use their knowledge of you to your disadvantage.

7. Do not expect anyone to console you or defend you if you are fired.

Those Who Give Ulcers Also Get Them

Top executives have a reputation for being unreasonably demanding on their employees. They are frequently blamed for everything from ulcers to headaches. However, the pressures they exert on their subordinates are often only a fraction of the stress they are under themselves.

Frank Adae, president of Blue Cross and Blue Shield of Kansas City, says, "I know I do pass down some of my stress. It's necessary if the job is to get done. I answer to two large boards of directors, and when they start asking questions, I go back to my office and also have to start asking questions. When I put my subordinates under pressure for answers, they go to their subordinates for the specific information. It's a chain reaction."

Another top national executive claims his response is hostility whenever he encounters a situation in which he feels the job is not getting done. His personal pattern is to take control of whatever position was not producing up to par, and stress is created because the person in that position resents having his independence and authority undermined. This also sets up a chain reaction.

Stress faced by those in decision-making positions reverberates throughout an entire organization. Employees may view the decision-maker as gruff or difficult to work with, but they are only seeing part of the picture. They do not see the tremendous burden of responsibility which goes with top-level jobs.

Perhaps the greatest pressure on executives today is the demand that business be run for profit, regardless of the economy or other conditions beyond their control. "A manager just has to produce," says Jim Paine, sales manager and former director of management training for Motorola. "You must heed predetermined profit margins or you are out of a job."

The high visibility of most executives adds to their pressure. The higher they advance in the hierarchy of a company, the more isolated and independent they become. Unfortunately, this happens at a time when they need emotional support the most. Their "fish-bowl" existence simply does not allow them to share their worries or do anything that might make them appear weak or inadequate.

Most psychiatrists agree that loneliness is the greatest problem executives face. Usually, loneliness is the result of becoming overly absorbed in work. If executives spent as much time developing family relationships as they do business contacts, they could have meaningful friendships at home that would dispel much of their loneliness.

Executives face a particularly challenging task of confronting stress on many levels, from personal and financial stress to business, legal, and societal stress. While they may enjoy their work, the overwork demanded by their extensive responsibilities will often leave them fatigued. They may pass some of the work down to subordinates, but the responsibility they have for project completion and success is something that cannot be delegated.

Reaching a high-level position does not protect an individual from the conflict of ambiguity. In the case of an executive, ambiguity may result from conflicting obligations. Subordinates may expect him to have the power to solve any and all company problems, but policies of board members or other superiors may hamper his ability to do so. A common problem among many executives is that they have the responsibility for many areas but they may not have the authority to take measures they might feel contribute to that success.

Insecurity of position is also a job stress not unique to lower positions. While an executive's position may be more secure than that of an assembly-line worker whose workload is directly tied to product demand, the decisions made by executives are so important that one mistake may lose them their jobs.

Thus executives often are directly responsible for many of the job stresses their subordinates experience. However, the pressures they exert on others can more often than not be tied to greater stresses they are experiencing themselves.

Dealing with Executive Stress

It is obviously difficult for the executive to cope with the stresses inherent in his occupation. Without sound coping mechanisms, the tensions would be impossible to deal with while still maintaining good health.

Here are some steps the executive can take to keep his stress under control:

1. APPLY SOUND ADMINISTRATIVE PRINCI-PLES. Planning and proper work delegation are important disciplines for any executive. Without sound principles and objectives it will be nearly impossible to eliminate overwork, excessive responsibility, and conflicting obligations.

2. RECOGNIZE THE ROLE REQUIREMENTS OF THE POSITION. Accept these requirements as part of the job; fighting them will accomplish nothing.

3. MAINTAIN PERSPECTIVE. This means acknowledging feelings of annoyance and anger. While frustration will arise often, admitting it will make it much easier to regain objectivity.

4. KEEP A BALANCE BETWEEN WORK AND RECREATION. The first step to this accomplishment is an assessment of work habits. Every individual requires a different balance of fun and work, and overdoing either one will impair efficiency. In some cases, altered work delegation patterns may be necessary if proper recreation is to be acquired.

5. IDENTIFY AND ACCEPT EMOTIONAL NEEDS. While accomplishing this is perhaps one of the more difficult steps in the process of trying to bring stress under control, it is also one of the more important steps. There may be a discrepancy between what an executive *thinks* his emotional needs are and what his

needs *really* are, so looking to past behavior for clues about needs is in order.

Normal needs for executives, as well as for anyone else, include the need to be competitive, the need to be liked, the need to vent anger, the need to be dependent on others occasionally, and so on. If the executive does not feel there are appropriate outlets through which he can secure need satisfaction at work, he should look elsewhere.

Family life is the ideal source for emotional need satisfaction. If this is not a viable alternative, other adequate outlets might be clubs, neighbors, and competitive sporting events. The important thing to remember is that any alternative chosen should be totally disassociated with work connections or job environment.

6. AVOID EXCESSIVE CONSUMPTION OF ALCOHOLIC BEVERAGES. One glass of beer or wine at lunch is plenty; hard liquor should not even be a consideration for the noon meal. One tall drink sipped slowly before an evening meal can have a relaxing effect, but anything more than that is excessive.

7. GET PHYSICAL EXERCISE. A regular program of physical activity or other leisure pursuits is imperative.

8. LUNCH AWAY FROM WORK. Arrange to take at least some lunches away from the job. Center the conversation on matters that do not concern work.

9. TAKE TIME FOR HUMOR. Many businessmen take themselves and their jobs too seriously.

10. PRACTICE LISTENING. Many executive pressures will be eliminated if subordinates are happy, and their anxieties will be significantly relieved if they can tell them to a superior who will listen. Listening involves more than just hearing; it implies attention and understanding.

11. FIND NEW WAYS TO MANAGE. There are a variety of management approaches geared to reduce job frustrations. Try them; you may find some will work better than what you have been using.

12. PACE YOURSELF. Just as your body cannot bear up under constant physical demands without rest, so your mind needs its moments of tranquillity. Pace your days and weeks to allow for an even flow of demands.

13. ALLOCATE YOUR TIME AND ENERGY. Try to leave adequate time between meetings and appointments in order to let ideas and decisions gel. Remember that *your* physical and emotional well-being is your most essential contribution to your organization. Be selfish with your time; don't crowd yourself with unnecessary activities or decisions.

14. BE SENSITIVE TO CHANGE. Look upon it as a common and positive experience. While you cannot always avoid change, you can often predict it, so reduce the shock by being prepared. Regulate the occurrence of voluntary changes and allow room for involuntary ones.

Middle Managers—Caught in the Middle

Middle management has its own unique set of stresses. More than in any other employment level, it is typified by responsibility without authority. Subordinates look to this level for action and answers, but superiors may inhibit a middle manager's power to produce these actions and answers.

Middle management is almost a scapegoat level where goals and objectives are often incompatible. These managers may be told to increase business on one hand, but they may also be told to cut inventory. They may be told to increase the work output and simultaneously cut the work force. They are expected to get work out on schedule but they are often not permitted to pay overtime.

Some psychologists feel first-line supervisors and middle managers experience even more stress than top executives. Often they are caught in the pressure of being asked to be a part of the decision-making process when they really are not prepared or qualified for that type of involvement. In contrast, others may be ready for active participation beyond the involvement they are currently allowed.

One marketing manager described it this way. "I have to implement plans I did not design, but if the plan fails I'm still responsible."

Middle managers, unlike top executives, do not have the power or facilities to accomplish many organization objectives alone. They must depend on superiors, subordinates, and peers for the co-operation and efforts that make their projects successful. Maintaining these three levels of relationships is a juggling game that may make a consistent pattern of behavior almost impossible.

Val was a middle manager who found it particularly stressful to decide what the proper balance should be in maintaining a good relationship with superiors and subordinates. He had just been handed down a directive which ordered him to change suppliers. He knew the new supplier named in the directive could not supply adequately large quantities of materials. Consequently, changing suppliers would make him lose face with his subordinates. He was caught between trying to maintain status with his superiors by loyally following their wishes and trying to maintain the respect of his subordinates by following the course he knew would be best for productivity. Finally, he worked the situation out by consulting a peer who could use the supplier his superiors suggested; they simply traded purchase allocations.

The role of a middle manager usually demands a difficult duality of delegating and doing. This again causes stress by introducing an uncertainty about how to maintain a good balance between the antithetical approaches to work completion.

Ned, for example, eagerly accepted a new promotion to a middle management post with a specialized construction company. He visualized his new job as an opportunity to try some new management philosophies he had while simultaneously getting out of a labor position.

Three months after starting his new job, Ned was called

in to the chief executive's office. He was told that his work had been inadequate and he was being terminated. Fortunately, the executive was willing to discuss the reasons for Ned's termination. As the conversation progressed, it became apparent that Ned had originally been given the post because he was a good field worker and the executive wanted a middle manager who would be directly involved with working on each project personally. Ned, on the other hand, perceived the promotion as a progression to a delegation post. When he and his superior realized his failure had been a result of a misconception of where the balance between delegating and doing was for that job, he was given another chance at the post.

A talent necessary for success as a middle manager is the ability to translate ambiguity into action and vice versa. The middle manager's superior is interested only in what is accomplished and is not anxious to hear the specifics of how it was accomplished. He will hand down a list of necessary results, but it is the middle manager's responsibility to translate that list into a system of actions that will produce the desired effects.

Whereas some levels of management have accessibility to a scapegoat if desired performance is not reached, the middle manager has to assume full responsibility for his unit. He is evaluated on the results of the total operation and is solely responsible for whatever happens. This makes him particularly vulnerable to sabotage if either a subordinate or superior wishes him eliminated.

Transition stress for a middle manager is generally more severe than for any other executive because it represents a major change. Since he is generally chosen on the basis of outstanding functional performance, this stress is augmented by the fact that his skills are not transferable.

The magnitude of the middle manager's transition opens up possibilities of major pressure being exerted by former peers and superiors. Former peers may demonstrate resentment at having been passed over for the same promotion. If they become the middle manager's subordinates as a result of that promotion, their resentment may translate into lack of co-operation.

On the other hand, former superiors may become new peers when the middle manager is promoted. Here again, resentment or hurt pride at not having been similarly promoted up the ladder may inhibit what otherwise would be a harmonious working relationship.

While there are many causes of stress in middle management positions, much of that stress may be eliminated by the style of leadership the manager chooses to use. If he chooses to experiment with various styles he will make himself unusually vulnerable. If he chooses to lead through the development of strong relationships, he must realize there will be times when he will have to face conflict in deciding which relationship will have priority.

The stresses of middle management may seem excessive for whatever rewards the position may offer. However, it is important to remember that pressures only represent challenge, and that challenge implies opportunity. The middle manager who is aware of the stresses inherent in the job can then face his opportunity objectively and make it a rewarding experience.

Breaking Out of the Middle Management Trap

If the middle manager is to manage the antithetical demands of the job successfully, the full scope of responsibilities should be defined. To do this, the following practices can be helpful.

1. DEFINE RELATIONSHIP NETWORKS. Determine the explicit relationship you will have with every person you will be relating to. Pinpoint the key relationships.

2. IDENTIFY REQUIREMENTS. This requires triple identification. You will need to know exactly what is expected of you in the respective roles of subordinate, superior, and peer.

3. RECOGNIZE THE DIFFICULTY OF ACHIEVING CONSISTENT BEHAVIOR. Triple levels of relationships may require triple sets of behavior. Success will involve balancing the three roles and admitting that behavioral trade-offs may sometimes be necessary.

4. COMMUNICATE JOB PERCEPTION TO ALL RELATIONSHIPS. Your understanding of what is expected of you should be communicated to every person you will have to relate to. This will enable them to understand why you must make the demands you do.

5. TAKE STEPS TO INSURE PERSONAL COMPATIBILITY WITH SUPERIORS. If you cannot establish

a relationship that includes values and goals compatible with those of your superiors, your tenure will likely be brief.

6. OBTAIN A CLEAR, CONCISE, AND UNAMBIGUOUS WRITTEN STATEMENT OF DUTIES, RESPONSIBILITIES, REPORTING RELATIONSHIPS, AND SCOPE OF AUTHORITY WHENEVER TAKING A MAJOR ASSIGNMENT. This will eliminate the possibility of having your job parameters changed without your knowledge later on. In a job where there is no scapegoat, it is important that you eliminate every possibility that blame might be placed on you.

7. UNDERSTAND THE CRITICAL IMPORTANCE OF CLEAR AND CREDIBLE COMMUNICATION CHANNELS. Absence of these will isolate you from realistic knowledge of what is happening above and below you.

8. USE CAUTION IN TAKING COUNSEL. Advice is fine, but the decisions and responsibility for them are only yours.

9. AVOID CLOSE SUPERIOR-SUBORDINATE RELATIONSHIPS. You should not allow intimate relationships to cloud the objectivity of decision-making or you may find decisions being made on the basis of feeling, not fact.

10. MAINTAIN MANEUVERABILITY. You should never commit yourself completely and irrevocably or else you may lose face if conditions warrant a change of course.

11. USE PASSIVE RESISTANCE WHEN NECES-
SARY. Open resistance rarely succeeds when used by
middle management, but stalling is often effective.

12. LIMIT WHAT IS TO BE COMMUNICATED. Some
things are better left unsaid if communicating them
will only cause anxiety.

13. RECOGNIZE THAT ORGANIZATIONS HAVE
FEW SECRETS. Things revealed "in confidence" are
seldom kept in confidence.

14. NEVER PLACE TOO MUCH DEPENDENCE ON
A SUBORDINATE. Few people are compulsively
conscientious, and the only safe time to depend fully
on an employee is when it is clearly to his advantage to
come through with the performance.

15. BE WILLING TO COMPROMISE ON SMALL
MATTERS. This will secure power for further movement.

16. AVOID BUREAUCRATIC RIGIDITY WHEN IN-
TERPRETING COMPANY REGULATIONS. Ex-
ceptions are sometimes necessary if subordinate relationships are to be successfully maintained.

17. BALANCE CENSURE WITH PRAISE. Pressure
from superiors may make it tempting to vent frustrations on subordinates, but the only way to win loyalty
is with generous amounts of praise and reassurance
where it is deserved.

18. BE RECEPTIVE TO NEW IDEAS. If you make others feel their opinions are wrong, your power will suffer. Listening is the best method of experiencing corrective contact with reality.

Take a Relaxation Break

"Mr. Franks is not available for the next few minutes," the vice-president's secretary said to a caller. "He's taking a relaxation break. Can he call you back?"

In another office, Steve Franks was sitting in an easy chair with his arms at his sides. His eyes were closed. He was relaxing.

For these few brief minutes he had put aside all thoughts of administrative duties to take a break from the tension and pressure of his job. And he feels he is a more productive executive because of it. He claims relaxation breaks leave him with improved thought clarity and increased energy.

Steve Franks has learned to schedule relaxation in the same way he would schedule an appointment or meeting with his staff. Many busy and overactive executives like Mr. Franks work under severe mental strain. Unfortunately, most of them feel that any relaxation which involves stopping work and sitting idle in an easy chair is a waste of time.

Years ago, Bethlehem Steel conducted experiments to test the correlation between relaxation and efficiency. At that time pig iron carried on the shoulders of workmen was loaded by hand into freight cars. An average day's load was a bit over twelve tons. Workers selected for the experiment were told to stop and relax frequently throughout the day. In a typical case, a workman who used 57 per cent of his day relaxing finished the day to find he had loaded forty-seven tons, almost four times the average day's load. An added bonus was that he felt less tired at the end of that day than he had felt at the end of previous days when he had loaded only twelve tons.

Recent studies have proven that the principle Bethlehem Steel discovered holds true in mental work as well. Lack of relaxation opportunities on the job is not entirely the fault of organizations. A majority of the nation's psychiatrists report that 75 per cent of their patients consult them because of an inability to relax sufficiently to release the pressures of the day. Relaxation, whether at home or at work, is something they simply have never learned.

Pace is the key to effective relaxation. Relaxation breaks should be paced regularly during the day so they can dissolve tensions before stress mounts to dangerous levels. A person who constantly works in high gear is likely to wear out sooner.

Pace also comes into play when determining work speed. Just as driving speed limits vary according to road conditions, the efficient worker will pace his working speed to situational conditions. Periodically during this time he will shift from accelerated mental activity to periods of mental stillness.

The Relaxed Breathing Technique is one way to accomplish the transition from mental activity to mental relaxation. It involves deep diaphragmatic breathing. When there is an abundance of oxygen in the system, muscles tend to be relaxed. Since a rapidly paced, tense person generally takes short, shallow breaths, his very breathing pattern inhibits relaxation.

To help slow your breathing down, breathe in to the count of five or whatever other count feels comfortable to you. Hold that breath for the same count. Finally, exhale to whatever count you have been using.

The heart muscle is one of the muscles that benefits most from controlled breathing. When breath intake has been slowed from the normal sixteen or eighteen breaths per minute to a controlled six or eight, heart action itself will slow down. The decreased cardiac action will give you a longer relaxation period between working beats and will ease strain on your heart by reducing its workload. It will also probably normalize temporary high blood pressure.

Regular practice of breathing exercises will bring about a calmness and sense of peacefulness throughout the day. It will also alter the constitution of the blood by effecting oxygen exchange.

The following exercise will accomplish the transition to gentle breathing. However, since it involves the lower abdominal cavity and upper thoracic cavity, it should be done on an empty stomach.

RELAXED BREATHING EXERCISE

1. Get into a sitting or lying position.

2. Put one hand on your stomach and your other hand on your chest. As you inhale you should feel your stomach expand. Immediately after that you will feel your chest expand.

3. Sigh deeply, exhaling to the sound "Haaaah" three times. This will remove all carbon dioxide from your lungs. Mentally put aside all thoughts and worries with each exhalation.

4. Inhale to the count of five. Pause five more counts before exhaling and pushing all air out of your lungs.

5. Breathe rhythmically through your nose.

6. During inhalation imagine yourself bringing energy into your body. As you breathe out, feel your body releasing all tension and worry.

7. Do about ten deep breaths initially. Gradually increase your number of counts during inhalation to ten, then take about twenty more breaths.

8. Let your breathing return to normal. Focus your attention on regular breath.

9. Observe how much oxygen you can take in during inhalation without getting dizzy; take in only enough to feel comfortably relaxed.

TECHNIQUE PRACTICE

1. At odd moments during the day, take three or four deep breaths. Focus all your attention on the relaxation of breathing.

2. Practice your breathing technique whenever you start to feel tense.

3. Practice whenever you have to wait for a stop light or whenever you are interrupted.

4. Practice after each phone call, and every time you look at your watch.

Coping with Organizational Strain

Organizational stress is common to every level of employment. It may be caused by company structure, but it can equally be caused by personality and temperament.

There are certain management policies organizations can adopt to decrease their employees' stress. However, when these are not available, the individual has techniques to reduce personal stress which can be used as compensatory measures.

The main way to relieve organizational stress is to provide for relaxation. One relaxation method involves taking a relaxation break and practicing breathing exercises.

Apart from the human concerns, companies are beginning to see that workers who are not tense and keyed up are more efficient on the job. The time is coming when it may be an accepted part of the office routine for employees to take a relaxation break.

STRESS ON THE JOB

Work Overload Got You Running a Treadmill?

Dr. Ray Rosenman, the noted cardiologist, claims, "The greatest stress is the one that keeps an individual constantly feeling impatient, constantly hurrying and giving him the feeling that he has not done everything he feels he should have done in a single working day."

These words describe perfectly what we mean by overload. Overload is not necessarily the result of others piling work on your desk. It can also come from an individual going after more than he can handle.

Stan is a young executive. He chronically drives past the speed limit, thinking he might save some time that he could spend in the office. Once there, he faces a mountain of papers and projects he is currently working on; he believes that having them stacked on his desk motivates him to get more accomplished.

Throughout his day Stan interrupts whatever he is working on to answer telephone calls and employee questions; he feels accessibility to his subordinates will develop his managerial potential.

He works until seven o'clock before calling his wife to tell her he will be late again. Then, grabbing a sandwich on the way, he attends a class he is taking so he can earn his Master of Business Administration degree in order to further his career.

To compensate for the time spent attending to interruptions at the office, Stan generally spends Saturday and Sunday working. He works as though he was being timed for a sprint race, and that is just about how long his body will last if he continues the practice.

Stan is a perfect example of an individual who creates his work overload. Granted, the type of work he is in could easily provide an overload situation, but he intensifies the potential and thus generates his own stress.

Monica, on the other hand, is working as an advertising agent. Employed in a high-pressure profession with constant deadlines, she works under a job overload very much out of her power. "When I have too much work," she says, "I can't spend adequate time to do things well. I have to take short cuts, and then I can't produce the quality I like. It makes me nervous when I have to rush through a job and not be able to have it come out as good as I know it could."

Others work with overloads that do have alternatives or solutions. David, an industrial engineer, works for a private corporation. Whenever he faces an impossible overload he approaches his superior so they can work out an alternative together. "If there is no alternative and I still have to retain the entire load," he says, "at least my superior will know why quality is less than what I usually produce, or he will be more understanding if a deadline is not met. Advising him ahead of time about the overload situation makes me feel much more secure in my job and keeps me from internalizing criticism for things I can't avoid."

There are two major types of stress: quantitative and qualitative overload. The latter occurs when an individual is given a job assignment that demands more extensive skills, abilities, and knowledge than he has. Quantitative overload is just simply too much to do in the allotted amount of time.

Quantitative overload is the most common form of work overload in this society. Programmed to be achievement-oriented, persons who grow up believing in the American dream often gear themselves to work unceasingly and feel guilty for accomplishing anything less than an outstanding quantity of work. And, if the individual does not always feel this way, chances are excellent that at least one of his superiors will. If that is the case, he may then be burdened with involuntary work overload.

In a recent *Psychology Today* survey on work attitudes, three fourths of those questioned complained about having to take their work, troubles, and frustrations home with them. All subjects said their work was basically rewarding, but they resented it when it cut into leisure or family time. As many as a fourth of those surveyed felt they worked excessively long hours, and more than another fourth believed they had to go to work too early or leave too late. A fifth of those surveyed said it was extremely difficult to complete work assignments in the allotted time allowed, and an equal number said their work schedules interfered with their family life. In this particular survey, executives and managers were those who complained most about long hours and the impact of their jobs on their families.

Psychologists agree that excessive overload leads to breakdown in any system, whether that system is biological or corporate. One factor has recently been studied as an indication of excessive overload as well as the signal that the potential for it exists.

Researchers John R. French and Robert D. Caplan conducted experiments to verify previously stated findings of the connection between serum uric acid and achievement orientation. They confirmed that the amount of serum uric acid in the blood definitely was higher for individuals who worked long hours each week. Interestingly, this substance is generally agreed to be the chemical which causes gout, and many men of prominence in history had it.

Work overload does cause other psychological factors besides gout. It is generally agreed that elevated cholesterol and elevated heart rate are results of it, and these in turn are risk factors in heart disease. Two psychological factors directly linked to work overload are job dissatisfaction and increased smoking, both of which are also blamed for increasing the probability of coronary trouble. It is therefore reasonable to assume that reducing work to a reasonable level will reduce probabilities for heart disease.

In several studies, men who reported that they were generally overloaded on their jobs were observed for work patterns. In almost all cases, they suffered significantly more interruptions from phone calls and visitors than their peers. In contrast, those who exercised more control over the workday had less trouble meeting their goal expectations and assignment deadlines.

Since overload, whether quantitative or qualitative, implies stress, it is important that overload be diminished if health is to be preserved.

Doing Something About Overload

Those who have power to diminish a work overload situation, whether for themselves or for a subordinate, can use a number of techniques to accomplish their goal. Some of these alternatives are listed on the following pages.

1. INCREASE TRAINING. If the individual can be shown ways to take short cuts in performing his tasks, or if he can learn new skills that provide greater efficiency or ease, his overload will be significantly reduced.

2. REDISTRIBUTE THE WORK. It is usually to the long-range advantage of everyone involved if redistribution of work is used as a solution to work overload. This will eliminate possibilities of work underload situations, a condition which is also production defeating. It will also improve employee relations by reducing workload inequities, and this will in turn lessen sources of resentment among peers.

3. TRY FLEXTIME. If work overload is caused by inconvenient working hours, one approach might be to set up a flextime system. In this program, an employee must work a set number of hours per week (usually forty), but he is given the choice of following one of several schedules. The factor here is that the schedule

he works under is then his choice and is therefore one which is most likely to fit his needs.

4. AVOID EXTRA WORK. Victims of work overload should learn to say no. They should resist the urge to take on extra projects by explaining they have already overcommitted their time or resources.

5. STRUCTURE TIME. Whenever possible, set aside certain hours during the day to return phone calls and meet with people. Hold a few hours "sacred" when you can't be interrupted by unexpected visits or calls.

6. ALLOW FOR ADJUSTMENTS. Every employee should be given the opportunity to meet with those people making excessive demands on him. He can then confront them with the overload problem and ask them to participate in finding the acceptable solution to his problem.

7. ALLOW FOR WORK DELEGATION. A structure should exist whereby an employee has the right to delegate or share work with other people if he is overloaded. He should also be able to ask for more work or responsibility if he is underloaded.

8. DON'T EXPECT WORK TO BE COMPLETED AT THE END OF EVERY WORKDAY. Accept the fact that there will be very few working days when desks will be cleared of all work. Being reconciled to the fact that all goals will not be met regularly will help to reduce the stress of work overload.

9. PLAN THE MOST EFFICIENT WAY OF COM-PLETING A PROJECT. This should be done before the assignment is ever initiated. Chart how much time should realistically be allotted for the completion of the work, and determine the priority level it holds in relation to other pending assignments. Avoid getting bogged down with trivial tasks which could be either delegated to someone else or reserved for a less busy time.

10. REMEMBER THAT THE AMOUNT OF WORK DOES NOT CAUSE AS MUCH STRESS AS THE MANNER IN WHICH WORK IS APPROACHED. Each employee should find the pace at which he can work with the most comfort and least agitation. This will considerably decrease job stress, even if a particular assignment requires long hours of work.

11. REALIZE THAT HUMAN PERFORMANCE DE-TERIORATES AFTER FIVE HOURS. Get into the habit of taking short relaxation breaks during the day. Stretch, do some deep breathing, look out the window, or find something else that will briefly get your mind off work. You will get much more production out of your time once you have had a change of pace.

12. BEGIN YOUR DAY BY ORDERING YOUR PRIORITIES. Make a plan of what you want to ac-complish and the priority in which these goals need to be reached. Begin by doing the important tasks as soon as possible. Take care to set achievable goals and real-istic timetables; resist the urge to list what you think

you *should* accomplish in lieu of what you know you *can* accomplish.

13. FOCUS YOUR TOTAL CONCENTRATION ON THE TASK AT HAND. Doing more than one thing at a time will only dissipate your energy.

14. DO NOT ALLOW OTHER PEOPLE TO WASTE YOUR TIME. This may mean cutting off non-productive conversations quickly or closing the door on unnecessary interruptions.

Not all these alternatives may be viable options in every situation. In some instances none of the suggestions might be applicable; in others, all of them might be practical. Keep in mind that work overload causes destructive job stress and must be alleviated immediately if employee health and organization productivity are to be maintained.

Responsibility: Getting Performance out of Subordinates

Responsibility is often quoted as being a major source of job stress. Responsibility has to do with being accountable for the results of a job, and when this is not totally in an individual's control he may find himself suffering stress involuntarily.

The more responsible you are for getting a job done, the higher will be your stress level. This stress may be partially determined by the type of responsibility you have.

There are two types of job responsibility. The first involves accountability for people in relation to their work, careers, professional development, job security, and increases in job status. The second involves accountability for things concerned with budgets, projects, equipment, and property. The first is thus basically related to people and the second to performance.

Responsibility for people generally increases as one moves up the status ladder. Those with this type of responsibility often become victims of work overload because they have to make themselves available for large amounts of time spent interacting in meetings and on the phone. As their responsibility increases, they generally find that the amount of time they can spend working alone decreases. Since responsibility for people is more unpredictable and less controlled than responsibility for performance or things, it is considerably more stressful.

Supervisory, management, and leadership jobs carry the highest stress potential of any employment situations. The social pressures of these leadership roles produce a greater physiological impact than even warfare. While those involved in war generally have outlets for the physical results of stress, those in leadership roles tend to internalize their stress more and more with every higher promotion they receive.

The accountability load of today's executive has a broader range than almost any other profession. He is responsible for choosing competent subordinates so he therefore will tend to blame himself if they don't meet expectations.

In addition to the variety and quantity of decisions he has to meet every day, he is also faced with the new emotional threat of job displacement. Just as the salesman-fund raiser college president has been replaced by a college leader who can interact with followers, modern demands are beginning to cause the displacement of the traditional businessman. These new styles of management and leadership only increase stress even beyond the previous levels of management pressure.

Today's executive is often torn between his wish to act autonomously and his need to share power. Whereas before, a manager was usually hired for his ability to wield power, today's executives increasingly must yield decision-making to subordinates or, at best, consult them regularly.

Actually, historical management values have not changed. The executive is still supposed to be in control. It is the mode of operating that has changed. Previously managers maintained control by authoritarian behavior; the same individuals now are expected to maintain control through diplomacy, psychology, and organizational devices.

Dependency on others to get the job done is not only stressful because it is the operation method in vogue; it is also pressure-filled because the executive often has no alternative. Today's technology is so vast and requires such a high degree of specialization that managers unavoidably have to rely on the advice of subordinate specialists.

The problem of too much responsibility is sometimes the fault of the executive himself; he may assume responsibility for decisions that could well be taken care of by subordinates. Consequently, the leader may be continually running out of time while those working for him are running out of work.

A negative by-product of managers unnecessarily assuming subordinate responsibility is that they also rob their employees of initiative. If subordinates can feel their manager will accomplish all their difficult tasks and make all their confusing decisions, they will lose their initiative for personal accomplishment.

The true leader *causes* his subordinates to perform at peak production. The most effective use of leadership is to ensure subordinates of confidently being able to say, "I did it myself."

In the best organization, people see themselves working in a circle as if around one table. In this circular structure, leadership passes from one to another depending on the task being attacked. This will create a climate in which all individuals can grow.

How to Cope with the Stress of Responsibility

Responsibility is an inevitable fact of leadership. However, ensuring that unnecessary accountability does not become a part of the burden requires careful guarding and planning. Some tips that can help eliminate this extra stress follow.

1. LEARN THE MOST EFFICIENT PATH TO JOB COMPLETION. This may entail training. For example, the foreman who is promoted to plant supervisor will be better equipped to cope with his new post than an employee from another plant. He has had at least some of the training necessary to fill his job description, and thus

the time spent in learning will be cut significantly. However, the employee from another plant would have the same chance for success if he received specific and sufficient training for the plant supervisor's job. Adequate knowledge will free him from making certain high-risk decisions and will free his superior from having to assume unnecessary responsibility for his success.

2. USE KNOWLEDGE TO ACHIEVE GOALS. You may know how to achieve a goal, but that knowledge is useless unless you activate it. If you do not have the ability to complete an assignment, acquire the knowledge that will give you the ability. Or, when dealing with subordinates, expect the same from them.

3. BE AWARE OF YOUR POWER TO CONTROL A SITUATION. Before starting a project, chart how much of the control for success is in your hands and how much is in the control of outside factors. Realizing that some things are beyond your control will help reduce the stress of accountability. If you evaluate a situation and find control of success is totally out of your hands, don't assume responsibility for it.

4. PLAN FOR THE UNEXPECTED. Have a contingency plan formulated to take over if another plan fails. In this way you can reduce the stress of failure by having an alternate route through which to achieve your goals.

5. SET ASIDE AN APPOINTED TIME TO HELP OTHERS. Make a joint determination of what the solution sought might be, and decide which specific individual will be responsible for implementing the solution.

6. TRANSFER RESPONSIBILITY TO SUBORDI-NATES. When you are helping someone with a problem, make it clear that you are not assuming responsibility for finding a solution to that problem. If you do assume it, realize that their problem has thus become yours. Be willing to listen, but don't be accountable for the solution decided upon if that accountability would not normally be in your jurisdictional realm.

7. GIVE REWARDS FREELY. Rewards should be proportional to the effort required and will thus commemorate efforts that matter.

8. HAVE CONFIDENCE IN YOUR DECISIONS. If you don't have this confidence, acquire more knowledge so that you won't be indecisive about your actions. Expect to succeed. If all else fails, lower your goals so that chances for success are realistic.

Working in an Age of Uncertainty

In such a highly technological age, no one can be quite certain about what changes may come next. This is true of the scope of society and also of the structure of business. The inevitable result is anxiety and ambiguity.

Anxiety about losing control is a common result of change. This anxiety caused by the changing forces around us is probably grounded in our biological nature. Whereas primitive man depended on instinct for survival, modern man depends on learning and knowledge. If his knowledge about how to control a situation is threatened, his physical reaction will be the same as if he had been a primitive man warding off a threatening carnivore.

The anxiety in today's society is caused not so much by actual change as by the uncertainty about what change will bring. If the change has already occurred, solutions can be found to cope with that change. If the change has not occurred, the uncertainty that accompanies its anticipation is more difficult to deal with through definite actions.

Uncertainty is as destructive an element in management levels of an organization as it is in blue-collar levels. Although leaders typically have a high tolerance for risk taking, they do not have a tolerance for uncertainty. The difference between the two factors is that, in risk taking, some of the facts are known; it is only the result that will be affected by those facts that is difficult to predict. In uncertainty, there are no facts to go on; there is only ambiguity.

Uncertainty undermines the manager's strongest talent: the need to control what happens. The stronger his need to be on top of things, the more likely he is to be susceptible to the anxiety of uncertainty. When this element of the unknown becomes intolerable, a manager is apt to deny and avoid the uncertainty, talk to others who may reinforce illusions about it, project rage over it, increase his compulsive need to work, or resort to panic. The latter recourse is especially common in men who feel the need to act; if uncertainty gives no clues as to what action can be taken, they will simply panic.

Although avoidance of uncertainty is common in all normal people, it is not healthy to prolong avoidance. Otherwise, we will allow the anxiety that results to push us into inappropriate behavior. The only effective antidote to anxiety is emotionally mature human judgment.

Closely related to the anxiety of uncertainty is the anxiety of ambiguity. One can cause the other. Uncertainty over the trend the economy is taking might cause ambiguity in the job of a laborer that depends on attaining supplies at a reasonable cost. Or job ambiguity may cause a person to become uncertain about whether he will be fired for inadequate productivity.

Basically, job ambiguity results from having inadequate information about how to perform. Whenever knowledge of expectations falls below a certain level, ambiguity results.

Individuals who find ambiguity the most stressful are those who expect the worst from the unknown. For example, Monica is a talented layout artist who functions best when she knows what is expected of her. She is working with a superior who says only that he wants a layout that will sell, but he gives no guidance as to what he thinks will sell. Monica is rapidly losing all her confidence in her own ability, because she never knows whether her layouts will be accepted or rejected, and she isn't told the reason for whatever action is taken. If she could just reason that, since her talents are good, her work will probably be acceptable she could decrease her job stress considerably.

Continual change may also cause ambiguity. Planned changes can benefit a company, but continual change may leave employees indecisive about how to use their knowledge in the changed set of circumstances.

Those who suffer from role ambiguity at work experience lower job satisfaction and higher job-related tension. Also, research has shown that the more role ambiguity an employee reports, the lower his utilization of intellectual skills and knowledge is. This ambiguity also lessens the extent to which an individual will use his leadership and administrative skills. It is obvious, therefore, that employees suffering from job ambiguity cannot make their best contributions to an organization.

Organizations with high levels of job ambiguity experience high levels of turnover. An individual who is uncertain about how to get ahead in an organization will be ambiguous about where the opportunities in that organization lie. He will therefore rapidly become discouraged and will be easily lured to another occupation which seems to have greater opportunities.

All job ambiguity cannot be eliminated in any organization. It is a fact of modern society. However, to survive, individuals today do need to develop cognitive styles that will fit new conditions. It is essential to develop a tolerance for change and new experiences, and a larger focus on the whole of a situation rather than the details that contribute to it.

Dealing with Job Ambiguity

Ambiguity and uncertainty are inevitable, but the anxiety that results from them is not. Several attitudinal and action approaches can considerably lessen the damaging pressure.

1. COMBAT THE IRREGULARITIES THAT CONFUSE YOU. Discuss job ambiguity with your superior; ask for a written job description. Recommend yourself for training programs and assume the initiative wherever there is an opportunity to do so.

2. ACCEPT AMBIGUITY. Appreciate it. Life would be dull without some suspense. Adopt a "so what" attitude toward the possibilities ambiguity presents; don't expect the worst from it.

3. RELAX. Take a few minutes each day to relax and be by yourself. Use this time to compose thoughts and feelings. This will help you react intelligently to uncertainty.

4. TRANSFER TO A LESS AMBIGUOUS JOB. Be certain to do this only after you have given your old job a fair amount of time; all jobs are ambiguous and stressful when they are new. When changing, steer away from those departments that are continually reorganizing and shifting people from one assignment to another. Also avoid units which do not have clearly defined goals.

5. BE AWARE OF YOUR ANXIETY. You can combat it only when you are aware of it.

6. TRUST SOMEONE. Have someone you can talk to as a confidant. Make it an individual who will reassure you about yourself, not about your project.

7. SHIFT GEARS. Be willing to let intuition serve you at times rather than always relying on facts and analysis.

8. DEVELOP SELF-KNOWLEDGE. Detect in yourself the responses that do not correspond to objective reality. Then search for alternate courses of action.

9. LISTEN. While a good listener will help you think out your problems, listening will also help you be aware of solutions others might have to offer you.

The New Battleground: Conflict in the Office

Ambiguity and uncertainty are not the only job stressors; job conflict is a major contributor to dissatisfaction and tension.

Conflict paralyzes many corporations because they feel helpless to do anything about it. Most administrators believe that every conflict situation is unique; therefore they do not feel past experiences qualify them to handle new problems of personnel conflict.

Some leaders feel conflict is healthy. However, they often fail to remember that there is no way to keep a small amount of conflict from growing into a snowball.

A particularly damaging form of corporation conflict arises when two executives let their competition grow into hostility. While hostility on the executive level rarely take the form of face-to-face combat, the paper wars they produce may be just as damaging. One marketing manager said his competitor carried out a yearlong memorandum campaign which never mentioned his name but did criticize his work. The campaign effectively damaged the marketing manager's style credibility and hence discredited his entire marketing approach. It eventually cost him his job.

Sometimes conflict may result in attack displacement. If the angered individual does not have available to him the individual or thing which is causing his conflict, he may find a substitute for his attacker. Fearful of a direct attack on a superior, for example, a plant foreman may choose to launch his attack on his superior's secretary.

Conflict as a job stressor may also be caused by conflicting demands. Many jobs may receive directions from two or more sources, and this is perfect for the development of conflict. In a typical office situation producing conflict, for example, one secretary is employed to work for three executives. Each executive may have a deadline to meet, but she is the only person who can meet it. In this way they are functionally dependent on her, which only aggravates conflict. If they cannot agree among themselves on the ordering of priorities, they may interpret the order in which she completes their work as grounds for competition.

A common example of conflict which arises from antithetical demands is that of the union employee. He may want to serve the company well, because the organization's success will determine the existence of his job. On the other hand, he may want to be loyal to his union, so he might participate in a wildcat strike which will harm his company.

Working mothers experience many-sided conflicts. Their perceived roles as wife, mother, homemaker, and employee may make demands that are in direct conflict with each other. This is particularly true when the woman holds a job that has a high amount of accountability. Research shows that in these cases, as in all cases of similar role conflict, the key to coping is restructuring the conflict and eliminating demands that are of lower priority.

One national survey of new work attitudes showed that as many as half of all employees are sometimes caught in the middle between two sets of people who demand different kinds of behavior. Fifteen per cent of these employees described the conflict as a frequent and serious problem.

Administrators typically suffer more role conflict than

employees who rank lower on the hierarchical ladder. The reason for this is that they spend less time working alone, and thus have more opportunities in which conflict can develop.

Bad interpersonal relationships often cause significant job conflict. While research indicates that poor relationships with subordinates do not always cause measurable damage, inadequate relationships with peers *can* be damaging. The reason for this is that subordinate relationships are not always perceived as threatening to an individual's job, so they therefore cause him little pressure. However, poor interpersonal relationships with peers or superiors may be interpreted as a threatening factor in status and job security, and hence they do produce significant tension.

It *is* true that not all conflict within an organization is necessarily bad. The balancing factor that can tip conflict into either a positive or negative category is the manner in which the chief executive handles it. A good manager will not try to eliminate conflict. He will instead try to keep it from wasting the energies of his employees.

Coping with Job Conflict

A major factor in coping with conflict involves dealing with the hostility that results. Consequently, most coping techniques involve ways in which anger can be vented, thus dissolving hostility.

1. ENCOURAGE DIRECT EXPRESSION. The employee who is allowed to express his feelings openly has found a verbal outlet.

2. MAKE AVAILABLE SOCIALLY SANCTIONED ACTIVITIES. These can often provide a physical, and sometimes psychological, outlet for anger.

3. PROVIDE DISPLACEMENT CHANNELS. Make available counselors who can listen to problems and thus eliminate the need for confrontation with the problem source. Provide a substitute target, such as a beanbag or other item, on which hostile employees can physically take out their anger.

4. PROVIDE FOR PHYSICAL ACTIVITY. Strenuous physical activity has tension-reducing value. This can also apply to anger that may need to be "worked off."

5. EXERCISE ENVIRONMENTAL CONTROL. Manipulating the environment may require providing new learning opportunities or simply removing the source of frustration or providing more positive or negative reinforcement, depending on the situation.

6. USE TIME. Removing an employee from the source of his problem will help the anger diminish over a period of time.

7. PROVIDE DISTRACTIONS. Giving an employee a difficult assignment which involves concentration may help him forget, at least temporarily, whatever is bothering him.

8. EXPLAIN. Uncertainty may be the source of employee conflict. Provide knowledge that eliminates uncertainty and you might also eliminate the conflict.

9. APPEASE. Saying "I'm sorry" may sometimes be the easiest and best solution to conflict. Apologizing recognizes the individual's right to be upset, but it also actively intervenes in the development of anger.

Change: The Technological Monster

Technology predicates change. While some do question whether change is good or bad, it is not actually change itself that causes problems. The underlying problem with today's technology is the rate of change. Whereas some companies used to take an average of ten years to introduce a new product, the average introduction time today is only two years.

Since the rate of change is so accelerated, much organizational attention today is directed toward the implementation of changes rather than toward analysis of human performance systems that go with change. Here again, most human systems are set up to handle change in itself but are inadequate to cope with the rapid pace of change typical in today's technological world.

Rapid-paced change eliminates the possibility of having time enough to develop systems that will handle change. Managers thus have to implement technology-caused alterations through trial and error rather than through a proven format. The uncertainty this causes is frequently painful.

The human response to change is many-faceted. Biologically, the natural result of it is stress. Our survival instincts become physical realities when faced with something that threatens our current manner of being.

Psychologically, human response to change involves questioning. Our immediate reaction is to question whether change will take something away or give us an opportunity for gain.

Technological advancement often dissolves established structures. While structure is less tangible than technology, it does give us a feeling of control and predictability. The loss of a structure will cause confusion until it is replaced with a new structure or system for coping with the environment.

Individuals usually respond to the loss of structure either by withdrawing or by acting out their confusion. Those who act out their frustrations initially argue, complain, fight, or even overwork. People who withdraw, in contrast, may tend to avoid people and work. They may sleep or watch television excessively, be prone to accident, or become negative and reluctant to expend any effort.

Reactions to the loss of structure are normal if they do not last more than a few months past any major life change. However, if this behavior continues more than ten months, the individual has failed to make a satisfactory adjustment. Dr. Karl Menninger and a team of psychiatrists with the Menninger Foundation have conducted a study of Peace Corps volunteers that categorizes their response to change into four categories, or stages.

These stages can be applied to any changes we make. For example, in a marriage the arrival stage is the honeymoon stage. Each spouse feels the other is perfect and that life is wonderful. The second stage hits in about six months, when they become more attuned to reality. In this engagement stage the young man may regret the loss of freedom from his bachelor days, or the woman may feel confined and taken for granted. In the acceptance stage they may openly express their anger and complaints, but each gradually begins to accept the limitations of the other and to adjust their expectations. This is perhaps the most crucial stage, since it involves the honest expression of feelings and communications. If they cannot resolve their situation successfully in this stage, they move on to the re-entry stage, when they separate or divorce and face an entirely new set of doubts and expectations.

These same stages hold true for professional changes, like a promotion. Even if the job is one you have looked forward to, apprehension and anxiety will be high. In a few months you will be likely to experience the second stage of change. You will suffer a decrease in motivation and morale and may suddenly realize how important the old familiar things in your past lifestyle were to you. You also will realize now whether you had any unrealistic expectations about your new job.

Unexpected frustration and the real recognition of losses become sources of unexpressed anger for many individuals. Unless they have an adequate way to deal with the anger and recognition of loss, they will become depressed and disillusioned. However, if they decide to accept the situation and make a commitment to it, they will experience the third stage of change.

The acceptance stage of adjustment may be more of a crisis for an organization than for the individual. Since it is in this stage that the employee begins to question company goals in relation to himself, he may abandon old ways of doing the job and restructure goals and priorities. Thus the company becomes open to close scrutiny and also has to cope with whatever criticism and complaints the employee may generate while venting his anger. It is very important that the company and its leaders be supportive of the employee during this stage. If he receives this support and is allowed to express feelings without censure, he will soon direct his energy into more constructive work.

Some employees experience a fourth, or re-entry, stage. In this stage they realize that their decisions have not worked out. This realistic appraisal of the situation usually comes after they have been in the new position for about six to ten months, and the usual result is that they return to a former position or seek another position with a new company.

The stages of change show us the process we go through as we work to restore our equilibrium. We experience these stages whether the change is joining a religious group, trying a new sport or hobby, or engaging in any other action that involves lifestyle adjustments. After the adjustment is made, we somehow find ourselves enriched, more realistic, wiser, and larger than our former selves.

This is the challenge of change.

Successfully Implementing Change

Changes of any kind become easier if the following conditions are met:

1. INITIATE CHANGE GRADUALLY AND AT A PACE THE PERSON CAN HANDLE. Schedule the

change deliberately. This will allow the company to be specific in its moves and suffer a minimum disruption of work. It will also allow for the unexpected.

2. MAKE CERTAIN THE INDIVIDUAL UNDER-STANDS WHAT IS LIKELY TO HAPPEN DURING EACH STAGE OF THE CHANGE. Treat each employee individually; don't trust explanations only to group briefings.

3. BEFORE CHANGE IS IMPLEMENTED, ALLOW EACH INDIVIDUAL TO PARTICIPATE IN THE DISCUSSION OF ANY CHANGES THAT WILL AFFECT HIM. The alternative is to allow employees to waste energy worrying about possible loss of status or responsibility, or possibly even loss of employment.

4. ALLOW EACH INDIVIDUAL TO EXPRESS OPENLY HIS ANGER AND FRUSTRATION ABOUT THE CHANGE. This will release energy for more productive work.

5. ANNOUNCE CHANGE OFFICIALLY. The first notice of change in a corporate structure should be announced via a letter to each employee at his office location. The letter should be sent from the senior executive involved in the change, or in a group meeting if facilities allow this. The announcement should emphasize reasons for the change and the impact it will have on the company's growth and profits.

6. MERCHANDISE YOUR OBJECTIVES. Implementing a successful group change demands that reasons for and expectations of change be frequently discussed and

advertised to employees. Articles in a company newsletter are an ideal way to accomplish this.

How Stressful Is Your Job?

The following quiz may help you determine how stressful your job is. For each statement, indicate a value of 1 to 7, with 1 indicating a low level of agreement and 7 indicating the highest level of agreement with the statement.

1. _____ It is difficult for me to predict what will be expected of me tomorrow.

2. _____ I'm always torn between requirements to get a job done and the needs of my people.

3. _____ I generally have more work than I can finish in a given period of time.

4. _____ I have very little time to get my work done because most of my time is spent in meetings, with subordinates, or on the phone.

5. _____ I'm never quite certain about what my boss expects of me.

6. _____ I often have differences of opinion with my superiors.

7. _____ I'm often asked to start on a new project before I have finished the assignment I'm working on.

8. _____   I am ultimately responsible for the failure and successes of my subordinates.

9. _____   I rarely have a good understanding of the scope and responsibilities of my job.

10. _____   I frequently have difficulties in handling subordinates and others.

11. _____   It seems as though I never have enough time to do the quality job I would like.

12. _____   I am responsible for getting many jobs done, but I am rarely given the authority to see one through to completion.

13. _____   I seldom have enough information to do my job properly.

14. _____   My job is filled with things that I really do not enjoy doing, especially administrative activities.

15. _____   It seems as though, as soon as I begin to understand all aspects of my job, a new set of policy changes is put into effect.

16. _____   Because of the demands of my job, I frequently feel as though I don't have enough time.

17. _____   I spend the majority of my time working under deadline pressures.

18. _____   I wish I had less responsibility for the work of others.

19. _____   I find it difficult to maintain the skills and information necessary to keep up with the continual product and policy changes.

20. _____   I don't think there is much I can personally do to influence company policy.

21. _____   Often, my job is too difficult and demanding for me to handle.

22. _____   By the time I go through all the red tape to get a job done, I lose the motivation and enthusiasm I had initially.

23. _____   The job skills I have now will probably be inadequate in a few years.

24. _____   I still am not certain what the criteria are for work and performance appraisals.

25. _____   I can't understand why the company wants to move in a new direction when the old methods seem to work.

26. _____   The most demanding part of my job is the frequent interfacing with customers outside the company.

27. _____   I am required to work with subordinates who are not as competent as I am, yet I'm still expected to get the job done.

28. _____   Some of the new directions and policy changes are being put into use faster than I can reasonably keep up with.

29. _____   I find it hard to delegate responsibility since I am never certain others will do the job right.

30. _____   I am not certain what my role will be within the company in the next few years.

To diagnose ambiguity, conflict, overload, and responsibility stressors, total the number of points you accumulated on this quiz. If you scored 30 to 60 points, the stress factors are low, and 61 to 90 points mean they are low average. Ninety-one to 120 means your job has an average amount of stress, but 121 to 150 indicates high average. If you totaled 151 to 179 points, you have a high stress level on your job, and 180 to 210 points is very high.

To determine whether your stress is caused by ambiguity, conflict, overload, responsibility, or change, go back and see which factor had the most markings. Questions 1, 5, 9, 13, 24, 26 pertain to ambiguity. Conflict is signified by questions 2, 6, 10, 14, 20, and 27. Overload is shown in questions 3, 7, 11, 16, 17, 21. Questions about responsibility are 4, 8, 12, and 18, 22, 29. Change questions were 15, 19, 23, 25, 28, and 30.

Stretching Exercises for the Office

An individual who sits for long periods of time will often get tight muscles from lack of movement. The person who takes time out from his sedentary day is often thought to be using up energy unnecessarily, but the opposite is actually true. Tense muscles use up energy and cause fatigue, so exercise actually guards against using up your energy before your day is over.

The exercises which follow are designed to keep the muscles loose and flexible throughout the day. The side benefits they provide are increased energy and a general feeling of relaxation.

These exercises may be done right in your office in the clothes you typically wear to work. Some executives like to do all the exercises at once, but you may prefer to break them up and do them at different times; it doesn't really matter.

1. JACKKNIFE

Stand with your hands clasped behind you. Begin by slightly arching your back. Slowly bend forward until your arms are reaching directly upward. Stretch until you can bring your head close to your knees.

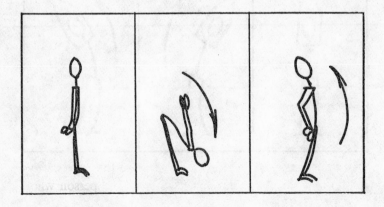

Hold this position for a few seconds. You will feel a slight pull on the back of your knees. Slowly lift up until you are in the standing position.

Start by doing this exercise six times. Later, increase the number of times you do it to more than six.

This exercise stretches the muscles in your chest, shoulders, and legs.

2. SIDE SWAY

Stand with arms extended and both hands clasped overhead. Your feet should be a shoulder width apart, and your toes should be slightly pointed outward. Slowly bend to the left, pulling your right arm overhead.

Feel the stretch on the right side of your body as you hold this position a few seconds. Then slowly stretch in the opposite direction, bending to the left as you pull your left arm overhead.

Do a set of three of these exercises. Later, increase your program to include six or more.

This exercise stretches your spine and waist.

3. BACK HANDCLASP

With your left hand, reach behind your back as far as you can. Grab your right hand and move it up your back from the waist, palm out. As you stretch, try touching your fingers.

Hold this position several seconds before releasing it. You may not be able to get your fingers to touch, but try to move them as close together as you can without straining. Repeat the exercise while going in the opposite direction.

The first time you do this exercise, complete a set of three in each position. Later, increase your quota to six or more stretches in each position.

This exercise stretches the back, shoulders, and arms.

4.   NECK ROLL

Begin this exercise while either sitting at your desk or standing. Drop your head and neck in front of you until your chin touches your chest. Using your chin as a guide, slowly roll your head to the left. Touch your shoulder with your chin. Pause, then stretch to the right side of your neck. Rotate your head until it is as far back as you can go. Pause, then roll your head to the left and touch your left shoulder with your chin.

Feel the stretch in the muscles on the left side of your neck as you hold this position. Bring your head forward and relax. Then repeat the exercise in the opposite direction.

Do a set of three exercises in each direction. Gradually work up to six or more.

This exercise relaxes the neck and shoulders.

5. DESK PUSH-UP

With your arms outstretched, place both hands shoulder width apart on your desk, with your feet behind you. Slowly move your chest to the desk as you press down, bending and pressing against your arms while you do this.

Pause a few seconds to feel the stretch in your shoulders and arms. Gradually, push your body away from the desk.

Repeat this exercise three more times. Later, increase to a set of six or more.

This exercise strengthens the arms and upper back.

6. CHAIR LEG LIFT

Sitting in a chair, point and flex your toes. Slowly lift your legs as high as you can without straining. Hold that position a few seconds so you can feel the muscles in your abdomen stretching. Gradually bring your legs back down until your feet touch the floor.

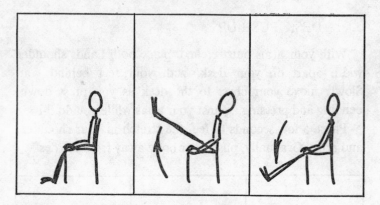

Repeat this exercise three more times; then increase to six exercise completions.

This exercise stretches the stomach and leg muscles.

7.   CHAIR SQUAT

Holding the back of your chair for balance, squat down with your feet flat and toes pointed outward. Pause to feel the stretch in your legs and lower back and then gradually come up to a standing position.

Repeat this exercise three more times. Gradually increase to six or more times.

This exercise conditions and develops flexibility in leg muscles.

8.   SIDE SWING

Stand erect while holding a book in front of you. Cross your legs, then slowly swing to the left. Pause and feel the stretch in your upper back and shoulders.

Repeat this movement in the opposite direction, and duplicate the routine three more times. In future sessions, do a set of six or more exercises.

This exercise stretches the muscles in the waist and side.

9.   BOOK LIFT BEND

Begin by standing erect with your feet slightly apart. To help give you balance, hold a book in front of you. Gradually raise the book overhead until you are standing on tip-toe. Drop your head and neck in front of you as you slowly bring the book to the floor.

Mentally concentrate on your back and shoulders. If you feel any tension as you stretch down, hold your body in that position for a few seconds to allow the tension to stretch out.

Relax and continue to hold this position. You will feel a slight stretch on the back of your legs.

Without bouncing, slowly raise your arms up until you are in a standing position with your hands above you holding the book.

Start by doing a set of three book lift bends. Later, increase to six or more stretches.

If these exercises don't appeal to you, try others:

1. Walk or jog in place for three minutes while thinking pleasant thoughts.

2. Walk up steps. Go slowly at first; then walk rapidly.

3. Row an imaginary boat.

4. Lift a telephone book with one hand. Then lift two books, one in each hand.

5. Stand on the balls of your feet. Press-push arms down. Fold each shoulder in and out.

Factors which create job stress affect the individual worker psychologically and physically. The personality characteristics of the job holder often determine the degree to which these factors create stress, but the sources which provide the opportunity for that reaction can be anything from conflict to work overload and excessive responsibility.

YOUR PERSONALITY—IS IT FRIEND OR FOE?

The Personality We Bring to Work

Jobs, in and of themselves, are not necessarily the cause of stress. While it is true that many companies create pressure situations for their employees, the stress that results from that pressure is highly related to the individual personality of each employee. Certain personality characteristics simply predispose an individual to experience more, or less, stress than his peers.

For example, a company may order the relocation of forty employees. In so doing it will create a potential stress situation for those being transferred. Thirty-eight of the relocatees will probably adjust to the move without problems; two will have personality characteristics which make it difficult for them to cope with the new situation.

It is interesting to note that some of the personality characteristics which are highly valued in business may not contribute to good mental health. However, these traits may be responsible for an individual's successful attainment of organization goals, so their detrimental aspects tend to be ignored.

Some of these personality characteristics are explored in the following pages. They really comprise a continuum. The characteristics at either end of the scale are extremes and hence are undesirable, with the only exceptions to that rule being the qualities of self-esteem and flexibility.

Few individuals will relate totally to one characteristic; overlapping of personality traits is normal. Most people will at some time or another exhibit qualities of many or all the characteristics.

A final thing to remember when reading about these personalities is that each one has competent coping abilities for normal situations. It is only when they encounter severe stress and pressure that some of their characteristics may be self-defeating.

"I want to be left alone."

An introvert is not very sociable and cannot easily cope with interpersonal tension from other people.

He is excessively vulnerable to injury, real or implied, from other people. Consequently, he does well when working on his own but operates with hampered productivity when forced to work with other people.

A good example of this personality is the patent attorney. He spends most of his working hours in the law library, rarely seeing other people except for an occasional visit to court.

Promotions trigger unusually strong stress for introverts being raised into a job description which involves working with other people. The additional responsibility is no problem for them. Rather, it is the act of being placed in the company of other persons that causes them to react with stress.

Introverts generally have a sixth sense about how much personal contact they can handle. Unfortunately, sometimes they are pressured into accepting a promotion because of the unusual creativity and efficiency they exhibited when working alone. A common consequence of this is that they can't do their work because of people distractions and pressures in the new job, and this failure causes depression.

A research biologist working in a rapidly expanding field was well respected for her professional success. Most of her accomplishments were solitary ones; she often devised schemes for evaluation procedures and designed programs for implementation of research on a practical level.

The biologist's work was so valuable to her employer that she was given a high-level promotion. However, the promotion removed her from her solitary environment and put her into a "think tank" situation. She was also expected to do a considerable amount of traveling while inspecting field stations for the practicality of their ecological implementation programs.

Job discomfort was caused by feelings of uncertainty about leaving her family whenever she went on trips, and by having to be in continual confrontation with people. Criticism was a major problem also. Whereas before she had no trouble dealing with criticism, which was in writing and which she could refute in writing, she now could not deal even with the constructive criticism that emerged in brainstorming sessions because the criticism was delivered in person. She simply did not know how to either perceive or counter criticism which was delivered personally.

Finally, the biologist realized her personality and temperament did not suit her to the job situation. Once she had identified the source of the problem, she could approach company officials about a change of position.

The only immediately effective solution for most introverts thrust into a social setting is the solution sought by the biologist; they simply have to remove themselves from the social situation. Independent by nature, the introvert may shun crowds because they tend to bring up role conflicts that threaten his independence. Therefore, this source of stress must be eliminated before he can return to peak productivity.

"Look at me; I'm here and I want to join you."

Extroverts are people who need people. They may need them because they seek the excitement and action that are frequently present in large groups of people. Some may need people simply because they like them and feel more comfortable when with people they like. Others may need attention and continual reaffirmation of their worth.

While extroverts will often work beautifully in jobs requiring the establishment of interpersonal relationships, their need of people makes them dependent on something outside themselves. This, then, makes them vulnerable.

An attorney considered himself very successful. He had status, position, money, and many acquaintances. Confident in his abilities as a lawyer, he decided to relocate and set up his own law firm with a friend.

During the first two months after relocation, the attorney

was extremely busy with establishing new client contacts and getting his family settled into their new home. He socialized with dozens of people each week, but the only real relationship he spent time working on was the one he had with his partner. When his partner died ten weeks after their office opened, the attorney was devastated. He had not spent time with his family, and his demand for socialization with a large number of people meant he had no close friends left. Faced with working in an office where he no longer had steady companionship, his work quality diminished and he slipped into chronic depression.

Extroverts work well with people, but they also *require* accessibility to other individuals if they are to perform even adequately. Confinement to a lonely job will depress them to the point of illness. Whereas the introvert will always be happy as long as he has himself, the extrovert must be constantly surrounding himself with other people if he is to maintain a healthy concept of self-identity.

"You'll do it this way or else!"

Perhaps the characteristics most difficult to change are those inherent in the personality of the rigidly structured individual. Since he is security-oriented and afraid to take risks, he would rather crack under pressure than take the risk involved in implementing a solution that has not been totally proven.

Rigid individuals are stressed by anything which upsets their routine. They are generally autocratic and rarely do well in management positions because they don't have the skills to motivate people.

Sometimes these individuals surround themselves with a

façade that implies they are well liked. This may in part be caused by their behavioral predictability. However, their insistence on knowing and controlling the details of everything going on actually inspires employees to work out of fear. Their reliance on routine and convention inhibits any employee independence and prohibits managerial flexibility.

Ben was a rigid personality who pushed his people long and hard. Regardless of whether anyone had a good or correct idea, he insisted that his formula for success was the correct one.

His subordinates had a high incidence of absences due to illness, and he had serious morale problems. He made sure that his work obligations were met, but he had to contend with a high turnover rate so he could never produce anything over and above the required minimum.

Ben's narrow, overstructured thinking and inflexibly autocratic behavior allowed him to get short-term results. However, his inability to cope with anything new or progressive meant his company had to deal eventually with long-term losses.

Since the very rigidity and inflexibility of this type of personality makes it difficult for them to change, behavioral rehabilitation for managers is rarely successful. More often, the only alternative left to a company that is partially or totally under this type of leadership is to remove the rigid individual to a non-authoritarian post.

"Sure, I'm willing to try it."

The flexible personality offers no trait handicaps that might increase job stress. Individuals with this personality have healthy, mature egos and can usually adapt to changing situations while tolerating a high degree of stress. They can generally delegate authority and produce well whether working independently or in a group.

Flexible personalities do have difficulties, but they have the ability to handle them. When a major electronics company decided to relocate to another city, most employees balked at the change. However, one engineer decided to present the situation to his family and discuss the possibilities relocation afforded. Intrigued with the prospect of new surroundings and novel opportunities, he flew his family out to inspect the new location and they collectively decided to accept the transfer.

The self-sufficiency of flexible personalities helps them take the disruption of a major relocation or change in stride. Although this does not imply that they experience no stress when presented with unique challenges, it does mean they will not increase their stress by resisting and dreading possible adjustments.

"Where there isn't any stress, I'll create it."

The stress-prone personality is hard driving and work-oriented. He compulsively pushes his efforts to capacity, regardless of what he is involved in.

He is extremely performance-conscious and goal-oriented, and he seeks honor and recognition. However, he rarely succeeds in finding self-confidence because he looks for it in the acquisition of an ever increasing number of symbols and material items; his sense of worth is based on exterior accomplishment rather than interior traits.

The stress-prone personality's ambition usually causes

him to overwork continually. He seldom allows himself to enjoy one accomplishment before moving on to the next one, and he almost always sets unrealistic goals.

One famous heart surgeon was a stress-prone personality. His schedule of writing articles for newspapers and journals was added to an already heavy surgical routine. His day usually started at four in the morning, but even when he went home around eight at night he would continue to stay up reading and writing for several more hours.

This lifestyle continued with no obvious physical side effects until his fifty-fourth birthday. Soon after that he had a coronary which prevented him from resuming his normal work schedule. He had figuratively burned himself out.

This intense drive to overload themselves with increasingly difficult tasks so as to improve their positions or reputations is typical of stress-prone personalities. However, by maintaining this pattern of behavior, they will almost invariably become candidates for physical repercussions, and they will be three times more likely to have a coronary in middle age than they otherwise would have been.

"If there is no reason to be concerned, I won't worry about it."

Being successful, ambitious, or work-oriented does not necessarily mean one is stress-prone. Much has to do with temperament and style of working.

The individual who is a stress reducer may be as serious as a stress-prone person about getting a job done. However, he will seldom become impatient, is less competitive, and will seldom feel driven by the clock.

This person works without agitation and finds time for fun and pleasure. Since he is aware of his capabilities and is confident in them, he is not obsessively concerned about what peers or superiors will think of his work. Consequently, he will not get involved in extra work just because it might enhance his prestige.

Sarah is a surgeon at the same hospital the previously described stress-prone surgeon worked at. She, also, is involved with publishing and teaching. However, though she starts her day at the same time he did, she spends time jogging or playing tennis before facing her surgery schedule.

When she leaves the hospital about six o'clock each night she joins her husband for an informal dinner. One night a week she attends a painting class; other nights she and her husband gather with a few close friends to play games or talk.

On Sarah's days off she will intentionally not wear a wrist watch so she won't be pressured or driven by time. She says this enables her to return to work the next day refreshed and relaxed.

Sarah is only a few years younger than her stress-prone colleague. While he has already overworked himself to the point of illness, she will be able to continue working indefinitely because of her ability to accept things as they are. Her talent for handling tremendous pressure without becoming irritable or impatient will continue to make her one of the more competent and accomplished surgeons in her hospital.

Whereas the stress-prone personality continually pursues his ill-defined goal of happiness through acceptance, the stress-reducer personality accepts what he is and can enjoy the happiness of his todays. He will consequently be able to lead a much richer and fuller life than his driven, exhausted counterpart.

"If I take a chance, I might fail."

Risk avoiders tend to be overly careful. They are forever afraid of making decisions because they are afraid a decision could threaten their security.

Feelings of inadequacy and dependency create a constant inner tension for them. This in turn restricts innovative thinking. They have a tendency to avoid exploring new ideas.

Risk avoiders seek job security rather than job challenge. They will avoid transfers and even promotions while clinging rigidly to whatever position has given them security and success in the past.

Greg was a risk avoider. He was just celebrating his fifteenth year with the weather service, but he really did not have much to show for it. He was afraid to apply for a promotion because he thought it might entail a transfer to another civil service office, and he had turned down several offers to leave the civil service for a job with an ecology company.

He ignored feelings of boredom that sometimes surfaced after another day on the same routine job. He admitted he sometimes felt small twinges of jealousy when he thought about some of the financial benefits his contemporaries reported having gotten with every move, but he just couldn't risk it. After all, he had his benefits and a steady income. If he accepted a relocation assignment he would probably fail and then all that security would be gone.

Greg sealed his position in life by refusing to accept the possibility of change. Like him, risk avoiders will even choose courses that in the long run are financially confining if an alternate course presents the remote possibility of failure.

"Hey, that sounds great! Let's risk it!"

The risk taker is the person who creates action where there would otherwise be none and who thus provides the fuel for most business and professional endeavors. This person is a logical thinker. He considers all the available facts before making a decision, but when he acts he is also ready to take risks.

Risk is a prerequisite to success for this type of individual. It is the factor that motivates achievement. However, the risk taker has such confidence in his decisions that he will usually be successful even if it is in spite of, and not with the help of, risk.

One successful marketing executive now runs a bass-fishing school. He used to work as a trouble shooter for marketing management and was considered to be an exceptionally capable manager. After several years of transfers and promotions he one day decided he would much prefer to make his livelihood fishing. His wife, as much a risk taker as her husband, agreed to the venture.

In the beginning days of his fishing enterprise, peanut butter and jelly sandwiches replaced steak dinners. However, now he is making three times as much money as he used to make as a marketing executive.

This situation could not have evolved had not the executive been a self-generating person who was willing to take the risk. It also could not have materialized if his wife had not had these same traits.

Tragedy can often result, however, whenever a risk taker is married to a person who is overly cautious and fearful of risk. The conflicts that will then result from their different approaches to life will be unending.

"They set me up to fail."

Outer-directed persons tend to blame the organization and others when things go wrong. They get their self-identity from affiliation with their corporation or work, and since this connection cannot be regulated internally, they feel vulnerable and helpless. To compensate for this problem, their immediate action when faced with failure is to produce all manner of paperwork which blames the group in charge of the failed project, and then to reaffiliate themselves with "the other side."

These individuals may be administratively competent in the sense that they can handle a great load of paperwork. In this way they can prove that they have been doing their job all along. Thus, anything that fails will be hard to pin on them. However, if this technique does not succeed in absolving them from blame, they may write volumes of justifiable complaints and valuable directions so they can then blame others for not acting upon these areas.

A highly qualified young engineering school graduate was hired by a large corporation. Lisa quickly earned company-wide recognition for her work. Since she was talented, capable, and ambitious, she soon sought and received a promotion to a first-level management position.

Lisa first ran into problems when funding for a project she was working on was drastically cut. Instead of accepting the disappointment and reordering her priorities, she blamed her boss for trying to undermine the project. "He set me up to fail," she claimed.

Remembering her last disappointment, she approached the next big project with apathy and lack of motivation. She tended to spend more time documenting reasons why it would not work than researching ways to make it work. She did complete the project, but the quality of her work was less good than she was capable of producing. Criticism from her boss only made her feel more helpless and unmotivated.

When she began to miss production deadlines and fail design specifications, her lengthy excuses no longer were acceptable. Management threatened to demote her, so she quickly resigned, claiming that faulty organizational policies and her superior's ineptitude were responsible for her failure as a manager.

Lisa never looked to herself and her inability to find alternative solutions to problems as the cause of her trouble. When she was hired, nobody stopped to think that success as an engineer did not guarantee success as a manager.

While outer-directed individuals *are* capable of success, they are quickly crippled by the least bit of criticism or implication of failure. And, since they are susceptible to spending more time documenting excuses than working on solutions, they only increase their own possibilities for inadequacy.

"I'm responsible."

Inner-directed people believe they largely determine what happens to them by their actions, attitudes, and inner resources. They are more adaptable and reality-oriented than outer-directed persons, but when under severe stress they will tend to blame themselves if things go wrong. Consequently, they may experience more stress than outer-directed people.

In extreme cases, totally inner-directed people can be shame- and guilt-ridden. Preoccupied with whether or not they did the right thing, they get lost in details and fail to see the over-all concept or problem involved. They become excessively introspective and obsessed with trying to find reasons and causes, and tend to analyze even small and insignificant items.

Larry was a training director for a large corporation when he decided to leave the firm and start his own consulting business. He had great sensitivity and insight into people, and he was good at what he did.

Although he had a fine reputation in his field and had contacts with other companies, Larry really didn't know how to start and run a business. Consequently, when he was contacted by several public relations people who claimed they could give him the visibility he needed to get started, he hired them.

Six months later, he realized his public relations people had generated very little new business. Angry at himself for being "taken," and disillusioned by all the money he had spent for nothing, he was determined not to fall in the same trap again.

During the next few months Larry became obsessed with trying to analyze the reasons why he had allowed himself to make such an expensive mistake. He felt guilty about losing so much money, and he began questioning whether he had made the right decision when opting to leave his former employer. Ultimately, he sought professional help and was gradually able to realize that his guilt and shame resulted from self-blame.

Inner-directed individuals like Larry usually experience greater job-related tension than outer-directed people. While the latter tend to externalize blame and assume that fault lies within the environment, inner-directed persons believe fault lies within themselves. Therefore, when confronted with conflict situations, they turn the conflict inward and thus experience greater physical symptoms of stress than their counterparts.

"Tell me I'm okay."

Under normal conditions, there may be no visible difference in performance between those with high ego and those with low ego strength. However, if stress is applied, the individual with low self-esteem will tend to be overwhelmed and show a sharp decrease in performance. This is particularly true if the stress is associated with having to learn new job skills.

It is unlikely that a person will succeed in the pressure-filled environment of business unless he has good self-esteem. The high demands for immediate results are simply too great for a low ego to handle. The inevitable result will be extreme depression.

Alice was recruited straight from college by a large company. She immediately showed signs of unusual intelligence and aptitude and was soon promoted to the first level of supervisory management.

As she excelled in her new managerial assignment, Alice was given an opportunity to relocate in a higher position at a branch organization. The chief executive of that branch liked her style of operation, so it wasn't long before she had been promoted through all levels of management. Eventually she was assigned to be manager of a factory employing several thousand employees.

Alice continued her success into the first few months of her new job. Then a previously reliable product began to suffer quality problems, and the generous praise that she was used to operating with was no longer forthcoming. As further problems arose which she could not readily solve, she experienced a sense of defeat. Instead of understanding the reality of her worth as a person, she interpreted her failure in management to mean she had no personal value.

If her sense of self-esteem had been internally regulated, Alice would not have felt so totally destroyed over the failure of one project. She would have had a transient sense of disappointment and loss. Although there would have been a process of grieving over lost hopes and fantasies, her recovery would have taken only days or, at most, weeks.

"That's all right; I'm okay."

Individuals with high self-esteem and a strong feeling of worth can deal with frustration more easily than those with low self-esteem. In fact, when this individual is faced with a pressure situation, his performance is actually likely to improve. He has a strong sense of confidence in his ability to perform, and since this sense of worth is based on internal qualities and not on external barometers, he tends to be optimistic in his approach to performance.

Maurice went from one job setback to another for the

first three years he spent with a national accounting firm. However, he knew that each situation resulted from something beyond his own power, so he never lost his confidence that everything would turn out well for him in the end. When he finally gained control over a project to the extent that he could personally influence its progress, he was extremely successful. From that point on he was handed one promotion after another, in rapid succession.

It is important that employers choose individuals with a healthy sense of worth for the management levels of their companies. This absence or presence of ego can play an important role in determining whether an individual can turn failure into motivation for success or whether the individual will take mistakes as measurements of his personal value.

It is equally important for each individual to be aware of his own personality factors so he can guard against the shortcomings that may be associated with them when under stress. This will help keep in perspective the real meaning of company crises and the individual's reactions to them.

Which Personality Type Are You?

This questionnaire is designed to help you determine if the personality you bring to work is the reason for most of your stress.

First, go through all thirty statements and rate yourself as to how you typically feel or react in each of the situations.

1=Never   2=Seldom   3=Sometimes   4=Frequently   5=Always

1. _____   Meeting new acquaintances is very stressful for me.

2. _____   My spouse or friends think I am hard driving and work too hard.

3. _____   What happens in my life is determined by fate and circumstance.

4. _____   If given the chance, I prefer to work alone.

5. _____   When a job is not clearly laid out for me, I begin to feel anxious.

6. _____   A negative evaluation about my work makes me depressed for days.

7. _____   I pride myself on accomplishing the most work in my department and being the first to meet quotas.

8. _____   Having to make business decisions is particularly stressful for me.

9. _____   There is little I can do to influence the decisions of those in authority.

10. _____   My work is less productive when I have to interact with others.

11. _____ I rely more on other people's opinions than on my own.

12. _____ I would rather have a steady income I can count on than a stimulating but responsible job.

13. _____ I usually work with frequent deadlines and time pressures.

14. _____ Since it is impossible to try to change a large organization, I tend to go along with things as they are.

15. _____ I tend to withdraw from people rather than confront them with problems.

16. _____ If one method for getting the job done works, I am not likely to change it.

17. _____ I need the praise of others to feel I am doing a good job.

18. _____ Since I do not want to fail, I avoid risks.

19. _____ I seldom feel good about myself.

20. _____ I become particularly upset with any changes in my routine.

21. _____ I personally do not reveal things about myself.

22. _____ I tend to become overly cautious and anxious in new situations.

23. _____ I have a tendency to produce more and more work in less time.

24. _____ Because of my work, I have no opportunity to do the things I really want to do in life.

25. _____ If someone criticizes me, I begin to doubt myself.

26. _____ I pride myself on being orderly, neat, and punctual.

27. _____ I do not like to go to parties or places where there are a large number of people.

28. _____ Luck has a great deal to do with success.

29. _____ I do a great deal of business during a game of golf or in the course of evening dinners with clients.

30. _____ I become particularly upset if I am contradicted.

If your score is between 134 and 150, you possess personality characteristics which are likely to generate a great deal of stress for you on the job. Your personality causes you to create much of your own stress, and this may limit your ability to function well under pressure.

A score between 114 and 135 indicates there is room for

improvement. This person is usually unable to handle high amounts of stress for prolonged periods of time.

There is a good balance between 74 and 115. You will have to make a conscious effort, however, to keep your behavior on the positive end of the scale when going through stressful situations.

If your score is between 44 and 75, it is not likely that your personality aggravates your reaction to stress. You probably are an individual who feels he can handle and control most situations.

A score between 30 and 45 indicates you possess characteristics which defuse much of the stress in your life. You have the qualities which make you a candidate for a leadership position since you function well under pressure.

The statements you just responded to can be used to indicate more than just how you react to stress; they can also identify what personality trait is causing you to react that way.

In order to identify which personality type you are, the items on the questionnaire are grouped around personality clusters. Add up the score of each cluster and you will see which is more heavily weighted. It is not unusual to have more than one predominant trait.

CLUSTER	PERTINENT STATEMENTS
Low/High Self-Esteem	6, 11, 17, 19, 25
Rigid/Flexible	5, 16, 20, 26, 30
Introvert/Extrovert	4, 10, 15, 21, 27

Outer/Inner Directed   3, 9, 14, 24, 28

Stress Prone/Stress Reducer   2, 7, 13, 23, 29

Security Seeker/Risk Seeker   1, 8, 12, 18, 22

Once you have determined which characteristics are creating your stress, you can begin changing those aspects of your behavior. The Behavior Rehearsal is one technique that has been proven extremely successful in helping you do this.

Becoming the Person You Want to Be

Behavior Rehearsal is a technique which shows you how to retrain your emotional responses to stressful situations and helps you become more like the person you want to be. It is a form of mental practice in which you rehearse success and prevent negative images from generating stress.

This technique involves more than positive thinking. It uses a type of body thinking in which the mind begins to associate feelings of calmness and relaxation in situations normally previously associated with anxious feelings.

Behavior Rehearsal can be used to develop positive personality traits. First you will imagine yourself already possessing the personality characteristics you want to manifest. As you do this you will get into the sense of what it would actually feel like to possess those characteristics. Remember, it is easier to capitalize on positive traits that are already there, no matter how small they might be, than to acquire what was never part of you.

This technique has been used successfully by business people, athletes, and other professionals.

Jean Claude Killy, skier and three-time winner of Olympic gold medals, used this method while he was recovering from an injury which prevented him from practicing his skiing moves on the slopes. His only preparation for the event was to ski it mentally. He reported that his first race after recovering from his injury turned out to be one of his best.

A corporate vice-president used Behavior Rehearsal to cope with his extreme anxiety about leading his company's national meeting. He began using this technique two weeks prior to his presentation and was pleased with his performance when the meeting materialized. He was even more pleased with his new-found ability to be comfortable on stage before an important audience.

Once you have decided what it is that causes your stress, you can plan how you want to see yourself behaving and handling the situation. The first step in Behavior Rehearsal is to write out a step-by-step plan on how you want to see yourself handling a specific situation that is causing your stress. Then implement the following actions:

1. Become completely relaxed by doing the relaxed breathing or muscle relaxation exercise.

2. Write out a script or visualize in your mind the person, place, or personality characteristic that normally makes you anxious. For example, if you are very rigid and inflexible, write that down.

3. Imagine yourself completely calm and in control of the situation.

4. Decide how you want to see yourself handling the situation. Be aware of what you want to say or do, how the other person might respond, and the results you would like to see.

5. Have several alternatives if the visualized situation does not go exactly as you expect the imaginary course to take.

6. Maintain a feeling of total relaxation in your body as you visualize the scene.

7. Visualize the scene several times while seeing yourself calm and in control of the situation.

8. Stop visualizing the scene if you feel yourself becoming tense. Take several deep breaths until you feel completely relaxed.

9. Repeat the scene as often as necessary until you can see yourself in the situation without feeling tense.

If you still feel yourself becoming tense, try this alternate exercise:

1. Imagine the worst possible thing that could happen.

2. Experience the complete intensity of the feeling.

3. As you bring up and experience your worst fears and re-examine them, they will gradually begin to lose their control over you. Realize this.

4. Begin to see how ridiculous it is to be dominated by irrational, negative feelings. Start to look for alternatives.

Risk Taking and Flexibility: Your Keys to Reducing Stress

Risk is something we will inevitably face every week. The stress we experience and the energy we expend in trying to avoid it, however, can easily be greater than if we were to take the risk.

If we are to allow ourselves the positive results of change, whether in business or in our personal lives, we must learn to take risks. Some guidelines listed in the next few pages may help you overcome your fear of this gamble.

1. DETERMINE WHICH RISKS YOU FEAR BECAUSE OF MYTHS. Are you afraid to have your in-laws over to dinner because they might not approve of your decorating tastes? The idea that all in-laws are bad is a myth. Nevertheless, you can trade off the risk of inviting them over for the smaller risk of inviting them out to eat at a restaurant. If you are still nervous, invite a few friends or relatives along so you won't have to be. the focus of your in-laws' attention.

2. ANALYZE YOUR FEARS TO DETERMINE WHETHER PAST OR IMAGINED THREATS ARE RESPONSIBLE FOR THEM. If they are past threats, realize that the probabilities of something negative resulting from your actions are slim. If it is an imagined threat, go through a Behavior Rehearsal so you will be

aware of how to handle the negatives that could result from your risk taking.

3. DECIDE WHETHER LACK OF INITIATIVE IS IN- HIBITING YOUR RISK TAKING. Determine whether you might be so busy anticipating risks that you forget to create necessary small ones. Take small risks. Read a book that isn't on the best-seller list; you don't always have to do what everybody else is doing.

4. DECIDE WHETHER YOU ARE SATISFIED WITH THE RISKS YOU TAKE. Balance your risks among professional risks, emotional risks, and personal risks. Realize that the type of risks you take and need to take vary with age and geography. The risk of traveling might have been a novel step in your youth, but perhaps the risk of staying home *instead* of traveling is more relevant to your current situation.

5. ANALYZE WHETHER YOUR FEAR OF RISK IS MOTIVATED BY AN INABILITY TO HANDLE ITS CONSEQUENCES. Take credit for risks that suc- ceed as well as risks that fail. Avoid castigating yourself when the results are not exactly what you hoped for.

6. UNDERSTAND HOW TO APPROACH RISK. While spending excessive time gathering facts is not always an appropriate solution, gathering a reasonable amount of information may significantly diminish the amount of risk actually involved in a decision.

7. EXPLORE YOUR OPTIONS. If one risk seems too great for you, perhaps there is an alternative smaller risk that would suit you better.

Specific risks may be threatening. It is only common sense to consider them carefully, but the concept of risk itself can be detached from debilitating fear. If this fear is to be handled constructively, the most important step is to face it directly.

Almost synonymous with an individual's adjustment to risk taking is his ability to be flexible. Some people seem to be born with this natural ability to adapt, while others have to acquire it.

Flexibility is essential for survival in modern life when changes in values and lifestyles take place at an astounding pace. Change has become a way of life, and perhaps that is the only thing we can be sure of.

If you have trouble being flexible, here are some suggestions to help increase your adaptability quotient:

1. LOOK AT EVERY PROBLEM IN TERMS OF ITS SOLUTIONS. Have several alternative solutions thought out in case one does not work. This will leave you more options and will help you learn the ability to cope.

2. Remember, AS LONG AS THINGS STAY THE WAY THEY ARE, YOU HAVE NO OPPORTUNITY TO DEVELOP FLEXIBILITY. The situation itself does not cause our stress. Tension develops according to how we react to our stress. Unless you learn how to cope with change, you will crack and break under the pressures of modern living.

3. DON'T EXPECT OTHERS TO TAKE CARE OF YOU. We cannot expect the government, our families, or our churches to take care of our welfare; that is

something we must do for ourselves. Total dependence on others deprives you of your power and ability to develop inner resources. You are the only one who can change whatever in your life is not working.

4. GRACEFULLY LET GO OF THE THINGS OF THE PAST THAT ARE NO LONGER USEFUL OR RELEVANT. Instead of rigidly holding to the past and trying to prevent change, learn to flow with the present. Rely on your innate wisdom to guide you; don't depend on rules and regulations for clues.

5. ACCEPT CHANGE. Realize that, while some change is good and some is bad, the world *is* changing. Develop the attitude that says the world is not moving too fast; people are simply moving too slowly. To resist change and continually uphold the status quo is to fight a losing battle.

6. RECOGNIZE THAT THE ONE THING INHIBITING YOUR FLEXIBILITY IS FEAR. Fearing a situation is *not* synonymous with being careful. Don't spend your energy protecting yourself from imaginary situations. If you are reasonably cautious, you should not allow fear to limit your actions.

7. CONSIDER MISTAKES TO BE LEARNING EXPERIENCES. One mistake should not make you fearful of every similar situation thereafter.

8. MAKE A LIST OF ALL THE THINGS YOU HAVE WANTED TO DO BUT NEVER HAVE. See if any of these can be done today. Get rid of automatic and use-

STRESSES AND STRAINS OF WORKING WOMEN

Stress Does Not Discriminate

Whether you are a woman moving up in a career or a wife trying to manage both job and family, you already know the meaning of the word "stress." The pressures and tensions it brings on are likely to show up through headaches, fatigue, irritability, clammy hands, indigestion, excessive eating or smoking, drinking, insomnia, or a variety of other ills. These physical symptoms will in turn have an impact on your work performance and your personal life.

Women who have entered the male-dominated corporate ranks have done so at the same price as their male counterparts. They have all succumbed to achievers' diseases.

Contemporary women are getting cardiac diseases as never before. Whether this is caused by job stress or by the accelerated lifestyle that goes hand in hand with big business is under debate, but the phenomenally increased rate of female coronaries, often at extremely young ages, is not questioned.

Women have been shown to react better physiologically under stress than men. Recent studies at the University of Stockholm indicate this may be due to the female hormonal mechanism for responding to stress, which is less geared than the male system for triggering the body's stress reactions. Other physicians contend that women have been more conditioned to be in tune with their bodies than men have. Therefore, they sometimes may recognize the signs of stress more easily.

The female physiological advantage for handling stress is balanced, however, by their increased competition. Since women are still in the minority in management, female achievers will tend to compete more strenuously than their male counterparts. The end result is that the rate at which women get stress-related illnesses is now almost equal to that of men.

Although results of female and male stress are basically the same, the dynamics which cause that stress sometimes differ slightly.

For example, women involved in a management situation in which all other executives are males frequently complain of the "fishbowl" syndrome. Their minority status makes them naturally more conspicuous, so their work is also sometimes subjected to more thorough scrutiny. Also, if they are on a peer level with a traditional male who has not yet accepted the concept of female management, they will be constantly watched for errors in performance.

One stressor that affects a great number of corporate women is the idea that they may have to work harder than their male counterparts if they are to prove themselves. In some situations this is justified; in others the pressure is self-imposed.

Perhaps the most common complaint expressed by working women is that they feel constantly fatigued and exhausted. "By the time I get home at night I am usually so exhausted, I have no energy left for either my family or myself," one typical woman said. "I experience so much frustration because of it that I've finally restructured priorities. Unfortunately, some of the things that had to go were things that made my job seem more rewarding."

The dynamics of corporate stress have their greatest differences in subordinate attitudes toward leadership. Generally, men have a difficult time knowing how to relate to female leadership; nothing in their conditioning has prepared them for a positive concept of female leadership. Some men will develop a mother complex. If they had a poor relationship with their mother, they might even make their female superior the target of their unresolved conflicts. Other men may treat a woman executive like a wife, sweetheart, or buddy. The perceptive woman will realize that her relationships with male subordinates will often be tainted by cultural overtones. Until she becomes aware of this, there is no way she can compensate for it.

Regardless of the dynamics involved, stress has an almost equal impact on men and women. Fortunately, they also have equal opportunities for reducing the physical hazards of that stress.

Women in Business: Working Against Stereotypes

Today's women have more options than any of their predecessors ever had. Whereas before their options were restricted to activities concerned with home and family, to-day's woman can choose from an almost endless multitude of alternatives.

Ironically, it is this very freedom to choose any of many lifestyles and life purposes which is creating stress for many contemporary women. As they begin to make decisions about how to live their lives, they are abandoning the confining but secure tradition of reliance on their male counterparts for any important choice selections.

Perhaps the biggest problem today's women face centers around culturally conditioned stereotypes concerning role traits. They generally can accept the contemporary role changes that concern men. However, it is harder for them to internalize role concepts of what the contemporary women should act like. This is comparatively easy to incorporate into verbal communications, but reconciling the changes to conditioned role perceptions is another matter.

At issue in the process of role reconceptualization is the very identity of woman. While she advances in business, she may have to change homemaking practices. If she cannot separate her identity from what she was conditioned to believe was successful homemaking, she will never be fully able to appreciate and use to advantage her professional accomplishments.

More than anything else, today's woman needs perseverance, strength, and determination if she is to survive as a person and maintain a positive self-image. She continually will face pressures from two main sources. One set of stresses will come from the cultural expectations regarding a woman's role. The other set, and perhaps the most difficult of the two, will be the internal conflicts created by her natural insecurities as she goes against a traditional life-style.

Perhaps the first barrier a businesswoman will face is lack of familiarity with how the male business network operates. Most women entering non-traditional jobs experience a cultural shock because they cannot understand the political and competitive structure. It is foreign to everything they were brought up to believe concerning acceptable female behavior.

For example, most women have been conditioned to show trust and approval toward only those individuals they personally like. However, business structure may require them to show outward respect for someone they deem incompetent so a projected goal can be attained or a political battle won. To overcome this barrier, they must realize that they do not have to like someone to work with him effectively.

Whether behavior that contradicts feelings is healthy is questionable; it is merely an accepted fact in American business today. Actually, some psychologists contend that what is considered healthy behavior is often determined by the cultural environment in which a person lives. One action may be viewed as healthy in one culture and neurotic in another. The key is whether the individual can reconcile himself to that behavior without conflict.

An important factor inhibiting a woman's effective entrance into the professional world is that she seldom has sufficient role models to follow. Since passivity, dependence, and lack of power have been the accepted behavioral traits unique to women, those who go against these stereotypes often feel something is wrong with them.

The concept of power is very important for working women to understand if they are to be successful. Traditional values considered power to be a male quality. Consequently, many women are afraid of it. They must nevertheless learn to use it if they are to escape from conventional roles.

There are basically two types of power. The first is power by authority and comes through the role an individual plays in his corporation (title, function, degrees). It is based on external circumstances and can change as circumstances change.

The second type of power is personal power. This comes from what an individual is as a person, his inner strength, and is less common than power by authority when used in a professional setting.

Women, like men, often ascend to a position of power only to find that it is attacked and questioned. And in some situations they must be prepared to have their authority attacked even more than if they were men.

It is not only the power of authority in women that is often challenged; their personal power is challenged as well. This will create both internal and external conflict.

While it is true that some measure of discrimination continues to exist in society, it is also true that women are frequently excluded from centers of power simply because they have chosen to reject power opportunities. Managers and executives commonly complain that they have many management positions open which they have tried, unsuccessfully, to fill with women. Unfortunately, it is usually only inner reticence which prevents these ladies from assuming power and success.

Success is another almost impossible barrier for the woman who has been trained to be passive and dependent. Taught to view success as a masculine option, she has been conditioned to believe that attainment of success and loss of femininity go hand in hand.

Some women resolve the success versus femininity conflict through a healthy re-education process. Others try to play down their femininity and become "one of the guys." When this happens, guilt feelings and tension about identity are almost inevitable. A third type of conflict resolution is practiced by women who think to retain their femininity they must turn down promotions. And another group of women cover their success anxieties with a disturbing aggressiveness that makes productive work virtually impossible.

Those who are not intimidated by barriers of success, power, politics, and stereotypes may still be inhibited by a need for approval. The need for approval is common to all human beings. It is the conditioned desire for all-male approval which handicaps many women. From the time they were little girls, the most cherished compliments of many females came from their fathers. As they grew older, this need for approval was centered on their dates and, eventually, lovers and husbands.

Some women carry their need for male approval into business settings. Not realizing that their presence in management positions will only foster competition, they perceive failure if they do not receive the type of approval they were conditioned to expect.

Since career women are not getting the approval from

men, they are learning to seek it from peer-level women. As they advance in their careers, they are learning the importance of developing their own support systems.

Support systems are important to the maintenance of healthy concepts of self. A particularly effective method used by an increasing number of women around the country is the cell of six women. The cell will gather about twice a month, or whenever the needs and schedules of the individuals involved warrant it. On the occasions when these women gather, they share professional successes, failures, and anxieties. Through the process of realizing they all have related and normal problems and stresses, they will reinforce one another's motivations for success.

As women assume more responsible positions and move outside the traditionally female jobs, they will face subtle pressures associated with the resistance of sexist mores and practices. Those who succeed in their professional self-actualization will develop an androgynous personality which incorporates both traditionally female and traditionally male qualities. Others, less secure, may succumb to the pressures of role insecurity.

Until women resolve their inner conflict about role actualization, they will not be able to experience the fullness of their selfhood. Instead, they will be plagued by self-doubt and anxiety.

The challenges in business today test the very fiber of those women willing to meet them. Many are emerging stronger and more competent than ever before. This is a testimony to the strength and determination of the human spirit. It is also proof that each of us has the right and the will to determine his or her own destiny.

Can You Make It in a Man's World?

Test your confidence in managing others by completing the following questionnaire. Use the scale indicated when designating how comfortable you are with each item or how you might feel if you were involved in the situation.

1. Feel very uncomfortable
2. Feel moderately uncomfortable
3. Feel moderately comfortable
4. Feel very comfortable

1. _____ How would you feel if you were expressing an unpopular point of view?

2. _____ How would you feel if you were addressing someone who had just interrupted you?

3. _____ What would be your sensation if you were stating your views to those in authority over you?

4. _____ If you were attempting to offer solutions to problems even though there is openly expressed disagreement with your ideas, how would you feel?

5. _____ Would you feel awkward if you were speaking in front of a group of strangers?

6. _____ How would you feel about using your authority and/or power in a manner that could not be labeled as "bossy," "dictatorial," "slave-driving," or "aggressive"?

7. ____ What are your sensations when you find it necessary to repeat a remark which others have seemed to ignore?

8. ____ How does your behavior feel to you when you maintain eye contact, keep your head erect, and use gestures while engaging in a conversation?

9. ____ Do you feel comfortable requesting an expected but overdue service from a subordinate?

10. ____ Is evaluating a subordinate's performance uncomfortable to you?

11. ____ How do you feel when you are expected to apologize for something yet refrain from doing so because you feel you are right?

12. ____ Do you feel comfortable receiving a compliment by saying something to acknowledge that you agree with the person complimenting you?

13. ____ Do you feel uncomfortable about openly telling a staff member he or she is doing a good job?

14. ____ How do you feel when a staff member brings a formal complaint against you to those in authority?

15. ____ How do you feel about not getting the approval of peers or subordinates?

16. _____ Do you feel comfortable discussing another person's criticism of you openly and with your critic?

17. _____ Can you easily tell a staff member he or she is doing something that is bothering you?

18. _____ How do you feel when you turn down a request for a meeting or a favor?

19. _____ Do you feel comfortable telling a person when you think he or she is manipulating you?

20. _____ If a staff member contradicts a request you made to do a job in a certain way, how do you react?

21. _____ How do you feel when you change your mind after you have allowed yourself to get maneuvered into a situation you intended to avoid?

22. _____ What are your sensations if you express anger directly and honestly?

23. _____ Do you feel comfortable when dealing with an angry staff member or client?

24. _____ Can you comfortably handle a subordinate who is giving you a hard time about a directive you have given?

25. _____ How do you feel if someone criticizes you on a job you are working on?

26. _____ Can you comfortably respond with humor to someone's put-down of you?

27. _____ What is your sensory reaction when someone criticizes you for an error you have made?

28. _____ If you give a staff member honest criticism of what you see as a legitimate mistake and he or she retaliates by criticizing you, how do you feel?

29. _____ How do you feel if someone unjustly criticizes you?

You can use this quiz to help you identify those areas which are causing you stress. Pay particular attention to those questions you have answered with a 1 or 2. If you have less 3s or 4s, the "Twelve Rules to Reduce the Strain for Women at the Top" and the "Female Stress Defense Guide" will be particularly helpful to you.

Twelve Rules to Reduce the Strain for Women at the Top

Executive women will invariably encounter stress. However, there are certain techniques they can use when trying to reduce the strain of working and interacting in a man's world.

1. DO NOT CRITICIZE A MAN IN PUBLIC. If you do, you will probably create feelings of resentment and hostility which may hurt your working relationship.

Avoiding public criticism does not mean you should not confront the problem. Instead, find a private place to discuss what it is about his performance which is unacceptable. You will be respected if you are firm and fair, although you still may not necessarily be liked. Adopt a new personal motto: "I'd rather be respected than liked."

2. AVOID SITTING BEHIND A FORMIDABLE DESK DURING ONE-TO-ONE INTERACTIONS. Most men are threatened by power in a woman, and avoiding physical reminders of this power will help reduce some of their discomfort.

3. REFRAIN FROM BECOMING DEFENSIVE ABOUT BEING A FEMALE MANAGER. While remaining aware of the difficulties men have in relating to a female boss, do not permit or reward behavior which is personally offensive to you.

4. CONSCIOUSLY WORK AGAINST YOUR PAST CONDITIONING OF WANTING TO BE LIKED BY MALES. You will deliberately have to work on your handicap of wanting male approval. Succumbing to these desires may be destructive to you as a manager and limit your personal effectiveness on the job.

5. AVOID SETTING UP A WIN-OR-LOSE SITUATION IN WHICH THE ISSUE IS HIS MANHOOD VERSUS YOUR WOMANHOOD. Deal with tangible facts. Go directly to the problem and avoid being thrown off guard by statements such as "You are a castrating, abrasive bitch, etc." If an individual says that to you, calmly reply, "That has no relevancy to the

problem at hand. We are discussing this problem, and that behavior will not be rewarded."

6. KEEP YOUR RELATIONS WITH MALES ON A PROFESSIONAL AND BUSINESS LEVEL. Avoid falling into the trap of becoming "one of the guys." Emphasize your competence rather than your personality.

7. CAREFULLY STUDY THE INFORMAL SYSTEMS OF BEHAVIOR AMONG MALE MANAGERS IN YOUR COMPANY. Know your hierarchy and the unwritten rules and games which affect personal relationships and influence promotions and decision-making.

8. ESTABLISH FRIENDSHIPS WITH OTHER TOP-LEVEL WOMEN IN YOUR COMPANY. Make a commitment to help and support one another professionally and personally. Track down and inform one another of job opportunities within the company as well as outside of it.

9. DECIDE WHETHER YOU REALLY WANT A CAREER IN MANAGEMENT. What do you want out of your job? What things are important to you in your life right now? How long do you expect to continue working? Where do you want to be five years from now? Realistically evaluate your chances of achieving these objectives.

10. MAKE A LIST OF THE WORK SITUATIONS WHICH CAUSE YOU TO BECOME STRESSED OR EMOTIONALLY UPSET. See what patterns

emerge. Do you react this way when you are criticized or when you are involved in certain meetings? Does associating with a particular individual effect this reaction in you? Once you can pinpoint the situation, you can begin to control it.

11. TRY TO FIND YOUSELF A MENTOR. Seek out someone who can advise you at critical times in your career. A mentor is usually an older executive with experience and good judgment who can act as a sounding board for your ideas. He or she should be someone to whom you can go for advice before making important decisions.

12. MAKE YOURSELF AND YOUR WORK VISIBLE TO THE RIGHT PEOPLE. If you have undertaken any extra projects or special reports, be certain that this is brought to the attention of upper management.

Decide what departments and job experience you need under your belt if you are to achieve your career goals. Aim for operating or negotiating positions rather than support positions. Your primary concern should be to avoid waiting to be discovered; do something actively and constructively to advance in your career. Move from a passive to an assertive stance in your search for career advancement.

The Double Bind of Working Mothers

Most working mothers live lives that include work overload. In a society in which few adults have been conditioned to divide household chores equally, marriages are rare in which both spouses participate in the day-to-day jobs of running a house and caring for a family.

Actually, only a small percentage of working women work for reasons other than financial need. Approximately a fifth of those who work are widowed, divorced, or separated. Another third of working wives do so because their husbands earn less than seven thousand dollars a year.

In spite of the financial necessity to work, women's incomes over the past decade have continued to fall further and further behind those of men. On the average, women twenty-five and older earn barely more than half the salary of the typical male. Employment experts claim one reason for this lag is that federal laws banning discrimination have not yet caught up to enforcement levels of the law.

Whatever the reason, the necessity to work combined with low incomes often deprive women of the option to not work full time. When this option denial is combined with an unavoidable responsibility for family nurturing and household maintenance, women are caught in a double bind.

One conflict for working mothers is employer attitudes. Employers are among the last individuals to staunchly defend chauvinistic principles. A recent survey of male executives uncovered conflicting ideas concerning male and female job abilities. Despite the women's movement and socially accepted changes concerning role definitions, the majority of American executives still believe contradictions.

For example, executives usually say they expect wives to make sacrifices for their husbands' careers but do not think husbands should have to make the same sacrifices for their wives. More importantly, they feel strong family ties will improve the quality of a man's work but that the effects of this unity on females will cause them to work less efficiently and develop disloyalty toward company commitments.

Until employers as a group practice attitudes that are not discriminating, the effects of federal laws will be minimal.

Pressures at home are the opposite side of the bind. In only a minute minority of households do husband and wife share responsibilities equally. Even in homes where both spouses share physical chores, the main responsibility of caring for children usually remains with the wife. As a result, wives coming home from work generally cannot relax; they simply face a new set of chores.

Guilt compounds the problems of working wives and mothers. Women who feel they are slighting their husbands or children by working sometimes attempt to become supermothers, superwives, and superhousekeepers. They consequently are left with too much work and too little time for themselves. The tragedy in this type of situation is that the added stress is self-imposed.

While guilt, resentment, self-depreciation, work overload, and conflicting demands catch most working wives or mothers in a double bind, the situation is not hopeless. As with every stressed individual, techniques to reduce the physical effects of stress may help compensate when the source of stress itself cannot be eliminated.

Ten Tips for Moms Who Work

1. STOP TRYING TO BE A SUPERWOMAN. Recognize that you simply cannot do everything. Since you

will never have enough time to devote to your family, household, job, or social life, unreasonable expectations will only increase your stress.

Decide what is important. Then set your priorities. The kitchen floor may never be immaculate enough to eat from, but you are likely to save yourself from becoming mentally and physically exhausted if you are not compulsive about house cleaning.

2. ORGANIZE. Good organization is one way to reduce much of your pressure. To do this, you may have to arrange segments of time when you can be with your spouse or children. Remember, the quality of time spent together is more than quantity. Most surveys find that even women who are home all day do not spend any more time with their kids than working mothers do.

3. PLAN AHEAD. Try to get as much done at home as you can before leaving for work in the morning. Make beds, wash dishes, and even start dinner. Some women find crock-pot cooking the answer to their needs. By planning ahead, you will be more likely to have time for relaxing when you get home after a tiring day.

4. SOLICIT YOUR FAMILY'S SUPPORT AND CO-OPERATION. Have them share some of the work at home. Discuss with them the importance of your work for you as a person. Make them realize that you need their help to succeed since you physically cannot do everything alone.

Ask your family for suggestions of ways in which they can make your workload lighter so you can enjoy more time with them. By involving the whole family, you are teaching them that you are a valuable person with needs and feelings. You are not just there to serve their needs. This will contribute to their growth and maturity.

5. SET ASIDE TIME TO RELAX. Don't worry about all the things that have to be done. Find a time and place where you can sit and unwind each day. For some women this unwinding period might be most effective if spent walking through a park; for another, thirty minutes alone before or after dinner may be the solution. Whatever you choose to do in your quiet time, make certain you do something nice for *you*.

It may take a while for your family to adjust to respecting your quiet time. However, here again you are teaching them that your needs are important also.

6. SOAK IN A WARM BUBBLE BATH. A long, warm bath at the end of the day can relieve much of the tension and pick up your spirits. Just lean back, close your eyes, and enjoy the feeling of comfort and relaxation. Let the warmth of the water soothe tired muscles and refresh you. When you finish, splash on some after-bath lotion. You will feel like a new person.

7. WHEN YOU CATCH YOURSELF WORRYING OVER THINGS, OCCUPY YOUR MIND WITH OTHER THOUGHTS. Take a walk, do some gardening, wash the car, watch a light, happy movie. Remind yourself upon waking each day that today is the first day of the rest of your life.

8. KEEP A DAILY JOURNAL OF YOUR EXPERI-ENCES. Write down your feelings and reactions to different situations. A journal is one way to get out on paper feelings you might normally keep bottled up inside. It will help you look objectively at situations by being available for perusing after you have vented the emotion of the situation.

If kept over a period of time, a journal will help you become more in tune with yourself, your feelings, and the things which are really important to you. As a result, you may find yourself eliminating from your life certain people and activities which tend only to wear you down or discourage you.

9. PRACTICE SAYING NO TO PEOPLE WHO AL-WAYS SEEM TO ASK YOU FOR FAVORS. It is usually the extra things you take on which can become overwhelming. You can gently refuse a request for extra work or a favor by saying, "I appreciate your problem, but I am spread so thin right now that my schedule won't allow me to take on anything else."

10. KEEP MINOR IRRITATIONS UNDER CON-TROL. If you allow every annoyance to bother you, you will be emotionally drained.

Does Your Boss Give You a Headache?

Nearly every businesswoman encounters stress on the job. While she needs a certain amount of tension to make her job interesting and keep her motivated, if pressure becomes too intense she is likely to experience physical pain and discomfort. Most often, the first physical pain she will feel is a headache.

Tension headaches occur when there is a sustained tightness in the muscles of the head and neck. The causes of stress in the office are wide and varied, but often it is the boss who, wittingly or unwittingly, is the cause of employee tension.

Bosses may cause stress by doing anything from imposing unreasonable deadlines to yelling at employees or clients. The multitude of demands they may make on employees can be faulted for part of the stress. Or they may require employees to act as peacemaking buffers between them and clients or peers.

A serious problem bosses cause for women is sexual harassment. When put in a compromising situation with a superior, women are generally so taken off guard or afraid that they take no action. Accusing the boss does not help the situation because sexual harassment is hard to prove. Generally, the best solution is to seek a transfer to another department on the grounds that, because of personality clashes with your boss, you would be more productive if working in a different area. However, treating the situation with humor can also be an effective antidote.

A frequent complaint among many employees is that their boss takes credit for work they do. The key here is to add a simple report cover to every completed project. At the top of the report write, "Prepared by . . ." Or attach a memo to the report or project which says, "The report you requested was prepared by _____ on _____ date."

In most offices the biggest frustrations come from people problems and insufficient time. Much of the tension comes from the difficulties many bosses have in understanding and working with people. Or they may not understand the amount of time it takes to prepare an assignment or project they might have assigned.

The problem in a majority of stress situations is not so much the fault of the boss, however responsible he may be for having caused the stress. The main accountability lies with the employee who passively takes the abuse, over-work, or other form of pressure.

It is unlikely that bosses will change, although attempt-ing to communicate with them on problem matters is al-ways a healthy move. The real solution will be to learn which situations can be changed, and then do something to change them, and which situations are so minor that it is a waste of energy to fight them.

You can generally save yourself a great deal of energy and frustration if you learn how to handle your reaction to stress. While you may not be able to change the situation, you *can* neutralize your response to it.

Female Stress Defense Guide

When confronted with a stress situation, try any or all of the following stress defenses.

1. DO A FIVE-MINUTE REVITALIZATION EXER-CISE. Sit at your desk with your eyes closed and direct your attention to your breathing. Follow your breath as it moves in and out of your lungs. On each inhalation say the word "I" to yourself; with every exhalation say

the word "AM." Do not try to force or control your breath in any way.

The "I AM" exercise helps quiet your mind and restore your energy. It returns you to the very core of your being and helps maintain a state of inner calmness even in the midst of noise and activity.

2. BREAK DOWN EVERY BIG JOB INTO SMALL COMPONENTS so it doesn't become overwhelming to you. Make a list of the work you want to accomplish each day. Have a folder or loose-leaf binder so that as you finish each task you can insert it in the proper slot. This will give you a sense of control over your workload.

3. RECOGNIZE THE SIGNALS OF STRESS YOUR BODY GIVES YOU. The signals may be a tightness in your muscles, nervousness, or even a feeling of knots in your stomach. These physical manifestations of tension tell you something is wrong in your environment or in your response to what is happening around you.

Do not ignore early signs of stress. Left unattended, they can lead to something more serious.

As soon as you become aware of tension, try to locate the source. Are you getting upset over a meeting, or is it a certain individual you have to deal with that causes these feelings? It might be possible that changes need to be made either in your attitude or in the job itself.

4. DO NECK ROLLS FREQUENTLY THROUGHOUT THE DAY to relieve the stiffness and tightness in neck muscles.

5. BECOME MORE AWARE OF YOUR SURROUND-
   INGS. By deliberately slowing down your walk and conversation, you absorb more of your surroundings and
   reorient yourself to a slower pace.

6. AVOID BEING A PERFECTIONIST. Put your best
   effort into whatever you are doing; then relax and don't
   worry about the results.
      By continually striving for perfection, you create ten-
   sion for yourself. Perfection implies unrealistic expectation, and perfectionists thus are hard to live with because of the excessive demands they make on themselves
   and others.

7. WHEN PROBLEMS BEGIN TO OVERWHELM
   YOU, TEMPORARILY REMOVE YOURSELF
   FROM THE SITUATION. Take a coffee break, listen
   to music, walk around the building, sit in the lounge.
   You will find that problems won't seem half as bad when
   you can remove yourself from them mentally and physically. Once your mind is rested, you will be able to find
   solutions more readily.

Stress does not discriminate between sexes. However, the
dynamics of the way pressure situations are carried out
may differ. Much of this stress is caused by lack of
awareness and passivity. Other pressures may be caused if
working is not a chosen option but a forced necessity.
   To cope with stress, women must be aware that it exists
and be willing to make coping adjustments. Whether single
working women, working mothers, or working wives, all
women have resources through which they can reduce the
damaging effects of stress.

STRESSFUL OCCUPATIONS

Why Certain Occupations Are More Stressful Than Others

Certain occupations are measurably more stressful than others. They are that way not so much because of the skills required as because of the responsibility or interpersonal contacts that the positions entail.

Many studies have shown that an individual's responsibility for the welfare of people dramatically increases his stress. This is physiologically evidenced by a proportionate increase in coronary disease as one's responsibility for others increases. Persons employed in these capacities typically have increased pulse rates, higher diastolic blood pressure, and even an increase in the number of cigarettes smoked.

Responsibility for dollars does play a part in the increase of stress, but significantly so only when the actions of that dollar accountability visibly affect individuals.

In most stressful occupations a great deal of time is required to be spent interfacing with people. In many cases such interaction is with people outside the individual worker's own immediate territory. This outside interfacing with the public has a dramatic impact on job stress.

While every occupation has its own unique stresses, the ones chosen for description in this chapter are marked by moderate stress over a period of time. Actually, prolonged stress is more damaging than brief, intense stress. It also requires a longer recovery time than any other type of stress.

In one study done on combat infantrymen in Korea, those subjected to prolonged though moderate combat showed changes opposite to those in men faced with brief, intense combat. The group who suffered prolonged combat tension, regardless of how mild that may have been, generally had low adrenal responsiveness and a shift in the balance of body salts. It also took this group more than twice as long to recover normal physiological levels as the test group who suffered short but intense combat stress.

The stressful occupations listed here are by no means the complete list. Rather, they are presented only as a cross section of the careers which typically create unusually damaging pressure.

For the Cop on the Beat, the Real Killer Is Stress

A major stress for policemen is the community demand that they remain calm in spite of whatever they may face. A policeman may be called on to settle a marital dispute, and though everyone else in the room might be yelling and angry, he is supposed to remain calm. Or, when called on in a robbery situation, the whole environment might be tense with fear, but the policeman is expected to proceed as though it were a normal, everyday situation.

Often it takes great self-control for a policeman to maintain this consistent façade of calm. When he is called to the scene of a fatal accident he is not permitted to show his emotions. And when the result of some violence requires him to advise someone of the death of a spouse, he is looked to for stability.

The problem is that, while the policeman is outwardly maintaining his composure, the normal emotions of anger or sadness may be churning inside him. And, as long as he is turning those feelings inward, they will be producing physical reactions.

A Los Angeles policeman says the hardest part of his job is telling a mother or father that a child has been killed in a traffic accident. "I always imagine it could be my child," he says. "You just have to become very cold and aloof if you are going to protect yourself from being affected by it, and that's very difficult. The only alternative is to just keep hiding your emotions, and it's practically impossible to keep all this inside of you year after year without causing serious damage."

Compounding the policeman's problems of stress internalization is the fact that he rarely can share his problems at home. If he is upset by a gruesome accident he witnessed that day, he often refrains from telling his spouse because he doesn't want to upset the family's time together. In a majority of situations, awkward shift scheduling prevents his talking about his preoccupations even if he wished to do so; many policemen do not work an eight-to-five shift that would allow them to be with their families at conventional times.

Shift problems have repercussions in other areas of family life as well. Few policemen are home during the hours when their children are awake and home from school. This makes it especially difficult to develop parent-child relationships.

The high degree of job stress makes policemen especially vulnerable to street temptations. Some individuals soon discover that alcohol can make anxiety seem less intense or that drugs can be temporarily relaxing. After all, if a drug peddler is arrested and only two of the four bags of drugs found on him appear in court, the truth about who took the missing drugs will rarely be told. And, if a policeman is patrolling a beat with several bars on it, it is a simple matter to "check them out."

The availability of prostitutes is a factor that worries many police wives. When it is so hard to find someone to unburden your troubles to, prostitutes can seem especially inviting to a lonely policeman.

Perhaps one of the biggest causes of stress is the paramilitary organization of police departments. Success in the profession is partially dependent upon accepting instructions and shift changes without questions. This is difficult even in well-run departments, but if an officer feels his superiors are corrupt or even simply inefficient, he soon develops a feeling of total helplessness.

Inability to communicate frustrations, helplessness, and availability of physically damaging stress relievers outside the home are all factors that contribute to an unusually high divorce rate among policemen. Statistics compiled by the International Conference of Police Associations (ICPA) show that the percentage of divorce among police ranks is more than double that for white urban males in general. One Seattle study pointed out that there was a 60 per cent divorce rate among police during their first three years on the force.

ICPA statistics reveal that marital discord is not the only result of police stress. When asked whether they noticed any serious problems among their five closest associates, police responded that over a third had serious marital and health problems. A fourth noted definite alcohol problems. More than a fifth of the policemen said their closest associates had problems with their neighbors and with their kids. As many as 10 per cent said their associates had serious drug problems.

Many estimates say stress kills more officers than bullets. Frustrated by unfavorable court decisions, news accounts they feel distort their actions, lack of proper equipment, and a feeling that they are unable to make a difference in the human suffering they see every day causes some policemen to commit suicide. At best, they succumb to diabetes, heart trouble, ulcers, and other stress-related diseases.

A Three-Alarm Fire Sends His Heartbeat Racing

Most firemen say their stress is both physical and mental, and that the two cannot really be separated. When an alarm goes off they have to respond physically by getting to their truck, and also by immediately having to cope with heavy equipment. However, that same alarm produces a simultaneous mental reaction. Especially if it goes off when the fireman is sleeping, it may effect a kind of shock reaction.

The physical and mental stress does not end with the sounding of the alarm. Actually, it just continues to accelerate. While racing to respond to the alarm, the anticipation of what might be awaiting the firemen causes significant tension. When they finally arrive, they have to cope with the physical demands of carrying extremely heavy hoses. They may even have the added physical demands, if the fire is bad enough, of having to don breathing apparatus that they know will last thirty minutes at best.

The psychological trauma involved in some fires is intense. If a fireman approaches a fire to find a hysterical mother screaming that her child is still inside, he has the added burden of saving a life. The same trauma may be present if the alarm signaled a paramedic situation. While saving a life gives him a gratifying feeling, inability to do so may cause extreme anxiety. For someone who has a paramedic training but has to face emergencies many doctors never see, the pressure to perform efficiently is intense.

Firemen assigned to ghetto or inner city areas have their own additional stress situations to cope with. While a fire may be raging out of control, at least one individual has to go through the anxiety of inactivity so he can guard the fire equipment from looters. Or, in extreme cases, when riot conditions make firemen the targets of bullets, they may even have to abandon the fire until they can obtain a police escort.

Since firemen engage in such strenuous activity, they do

have a means for venting their frustrations. However, this activity may be as much a danger to them as the anxiety would have been. The high demands made on performance can motivate them to work so fast that their cardiovascular systems simply cannot stand up under the pressure.

Like a policeman's, a fireman's stress extends over into the family life. He usually works twenty-four hours and is off twenty-four hours. Consequently, the family of fire fighters he works with may become as close to him as his physical family. This can breed jealousy and competition. The stress of living in two different societies may sometimes even cause firemen to forsake one for the other.

According to the National Fire Prevention and Control Administration in Washington, D.C., the mortality rate among fire fighters is one of the highest for any occupation. An important factor in this is stress, because as many as 45 per cent of these deaths are caused by heart attacks.

In order to combat the alarmingly high incidence of heart disease among firemen, many departments have initiated mandatory physical fitness programs. Some are using the Canadian Air Force plan for physical fitness because it is geared to allow for age differences and deals not only with skeletal muscles but also with the cardiovascular system.

The vast majority of fire fighters applaud the new physical fitness program. They are tested periodically to make certain they meet the standards required of them by age.

While the institution of a physical fitness program is not the cure-all for firemen's stress, it will go a way toward reducing the physical damage caused by that stress.

Air Traffic Controllers: One Mistake Can Be Deadly

The threat of what *could* happen provides the greatest stress for air traffic controllers. Especially in the busy airports of Chicago, Los Angeles, Atlanta, Denver, and other major traffic cities, air traffic controllers may have to direct a landing every thirty seconds. Near misses become everyday occurrences, but the effects of those misses on controllers are not nearly so casual. The trauma experienced after having allowed what could have been death for hundreds may be the same as the trauma a controller might have experienced if the crash had actually occurred.

A great deal of air controller job stress comes directly from the employer. Traditionally men who make decisions in an instant, it is difficult for controllers to understand the slow progress and time involved in the making of an FAA decision.

Job stress is intense for the controller, but the way in which he handles it may be a prime cause of stress-related illness. The confidence needed to handle numerous and frequent important decisions requires a strong ego. Therefore it is difficult for him to admit failure or any type of physical inability to cope with the pressure.

Ulcers are the most common immediate form of physical stress indicators among controllers. At O'Hare International Airport in Chicago, more than two thirds of the controllers at any given time will generally be suffering from ulcers or showing symptoms of them. Large cookie jars filled with antacid tablets grace several tables and shelves in the air traffic control tower.

Few air traffic controllers are more than thirty-five years old; they simply cannot take the pressure for too long a time. Five years is considered a long tenure at any one of the busy airports; two years is more typical.

Since the job is so filled with pressure, recruiting for new controllers is difficult. Many come straight from military ranks. Some have college degrees, while others are drop-outs. The only thing they have in common is unusual intelligence combined with a daring spirit and an ability to make split-second decisions.

Air traffic controllers have so many stress-related illnesses that they are virtually impossible to insure for disability. Some estimates place early retirement caused by medical problems as high as 95 per cent.

Of course, disability is not totally to the disadvantage of the controller. FAA rulings determine that 90 per cent of his salary is tax-free if he is suffering from a job-related illness. If that illness prevents him from carrying out his job satisfactorily, he qualifies for two years of second-career training. The latter, however, is generally accepted only reluctantly; the strong ego of the controller interprets this as failure.

Like policemen, air traffic controllers have a high divorce rate. The frequent transfers and high tension simply do not help in the development of interpersonal relationships. More destructive than that, however, is the high incidence of alcoholism, drugs, and carousing that are the results of seeking anxiety relief.

Despite the low chances of establishing any kind of longevity as an air traffic controller, some individuals do manage to have long careers. When asked for the secret to their success, most agree that continually acquiring knowledge about their jobs, getting regular exercise, keeping weight down, and developing a cold, hard attitude toward consequences of mistakes are instrumental. "I just love my job," one controller said. "And, like everyone else, I keep thinking that physical disability just won't happen to me."

Playing for High Stakes: Professional Football Coaching

The stress among professional coaches is often caused by their inability to do anything once a game starts. They may have worked hard in the time preceding the game to prepare their players, but once the players are on the field the coach is faced with a situation in which he has responsibility for the outcome yet doesn't have full and direct control over the factors affecting that outcome.

Professional coaches do experience pressure from causes other than helplessness. However, the stressors are still related. For example, angry fans or angry team owners may cause stress. This stress is not the same as the stress of helplessness, but it certainly does make helplessness more painful.

Some coaches cite job insecurity as a major stress. This, also, is related to helplessness. Their jobs may depend upon a team record. Since some teams have to lose each season, this leaves a minority of the coaches with a record conducive to job security.

In some situations, winning a majority of games does not always secure a coach's job. With teams who make the play-offs regularly, nothing short of a season championship is considered adequate.

The ability to handle wins and losses with the least amount of emotion is often referred to as an important key in reducing job stress. A coach who wins must refrain from basking in his victory or he may miss the opportunity to categorize factors that determined the win. However, he must enjoy the win enough to avoid the depression that may result from increased expectations; fans and owners observing a win will generally expect improved performance and an even greater win at the next game.

Balance is also the key to handling losses. While it is normal and good to scrutinize game statistics for indications of what caused the loss, communicating this information should allow for maintenance of team morale. This morale is already low after a loss; using the wrong approach in pointing out errors will only cause it to drop lower.

Perhaps the most important factor in determining a coach's ability to handle job stress is his sense of self-esteem. In this age of television, radio, and extensive sports coverage, fans learn about coach or player mistakes as soon as they happen. Complaints generally are louder than compliments in these situations, so a coach needs to base his sense of worth in self rather than in performance. This does not imply that he should ignore the fans' comments; he should merely be able to consider them objectively.

As the sports orientation of this health-conscious society increases, the pressure on coaches will continue to increase.

The way in which they handle this stress may ultimately be determined by the maturity of their self-concept.

When the Dow Jones Goes Down, His Stress Goes Up

Stockbroker stress is caused primarily by the need to make a sale. Since income is derived entirely from sales commissions, this need is a very basic one.

The factors involved in making a sale, however, are not basic; they are ambiguous. Fluctuating political stability, the health of the President, or any rumors that might affect confidence in a company or the economy as a whole will affect the stock market.

The ambiguity about how to make a decision increases the stress of deciding which company to back. Although the money that might be lost in a bad sale might not belong to the broker, the commissions that might be lost if a mistake causes the loss of a client will affect him directly.

The highly paced environment a stockbroker works in also causes stress. Decision-making must be instantaneous, and events transpire so quickly that often he can go through an entire day without having had time for a break. After working in high gear for such a long period of time it is hard to relax.

Risk taking is an integral part of stockbroking. Part of the risk can be anticipated through accumulation of knowledge, but the balance of it simply cannot be charted.

Client opinions have a more direct affect on stockbrokers than on members of any other profession. A dissatisfied customer may threaten to complain to the Securities and Exchange Commission, and his complaint may have a result equivalent to the disbarment of a lawyer. Hence, while the income insecurity caused by relying on commissions causes stress, the ease with which a broker's license can be lost produces even greater stress.

The quantity of money and of customers a stockbroker must deal with during the course of a day further compounds his tension. He has to remember a variety of facts and remain versatile enough in his behavior to be able to satisfy the whims of all his customers. And, while some customers may call regularly to ask questions and get advice, he still cannot make any income off the lost time unless the contact results in a sale.

The most successful tool for eliminating stockbroker job stress is knowledge. The more knowledge a stockbroker can obtain concerning the stocks he is dealing with, the less risk will be involved in his decisions and the more confidence he can display in making a sale.

He's at the Mercy of the Weather, Fluctuating Farm Prices, and Government Regulations

Farmers live in a constant aura of uncertainty. They are subject to weather conditions that can never be totally predicted and to government regulations designed by individuals who often know little about farming. They have to operate with unpredictable machinery and fertilizer costs, and they often have to rely on untried workers who are inadequate for the job.

Debt is an additional factor that looms large in the picture of a farmer's stress. Working in a capital-intensive industry, he is frequently forced to mortgage his farm and live with the worry of wondering whether he will be able to meet the payments.

Physical hazards are another pressure factor for the farmer. Dealing with large and sophisticated equipment increases the probability of serious accidents. Even more hazardous, however, are the chemicals he must constantly handle. Some are so potent that contact between skin and chemical may occasionally have fatal results.

Risk taking also enters into the picture of farmer stress. On the occasions when weather and facilities have allowed him to harvest a good crop, he is still at the mercy of the economy. The indecision about whether to sell a crop as soon as it is harvested or to wait a few months on the chance that prices will improve is one that has to be faced continually.

Along with uncertainty, a farmer is plagued with inability to effect desired results. Whereas, in other professions, business measures can be taken to reduce stress, this is not possible in the contemporary agricultural community. The only measure he could use to reduce stress would be to reduce costs, and in today's inflationary society that is almost impossible.

Some farmers escaped from the city to agricultural life because they liked the fresh air. It wasn't that the business of farming was so good, they said, but that city life was so bad. Now, many of them are finding that the physical impact of farm stress may be just as damaging as the pressures of a city job.

Pain: A Part of the Dentist's Daily Routine

Suicide is more common among dentists than among any other group. Some psychologists attribute this to loneliness, others to the constant exposure to hostile patients who fear the pain they believe the dentists impose.

Whatever the cause, there is clearly an unusual amount of stress in the dental profession.

One cause is the pressure of time. With overhead costs skyrocketing, the dentist has to squeeze a maximum number of patients into his workday. Even on a full day, overhead may be as high as 80 per cent of what he collects. Thus he is constantly pressured with the conflict of cutting down on time when he would prefer to have more time so he could do a better job.

Space is a dental stressor as well. Working in a tiny cubicle all day and having to focus in on small details in a confined area creates a pressure all its own.

Perhaps the most stressful attribute of dentists' pressure is that it is prolonged. Whereas a surgeon may have to perform an intense two-hour surgery, a dentist performs comparably difficult work for eight or more hours in a day.

Patient attitudes are often cited as being responsible for dentists' feelings of alienation. One of the ironies of the profession is that patients pay for pain, because pain is produced in the process of remedying problems. Thus a dentist is usually thought of in association with the pain that prompts a patient to visit him as well as the pain he causes in the process of treating the patient. Compliments, regardless of how well they might be deserved, are consequently few and far between.

The dentists who get involved in suicide crisis situations are frequently the individuals who are so occupied with their work and its stresses that they don't develop avenues in which to release tension. Those who jog, play tennis or other sports, and those who find a confidant with whom they can discuss anxieties generally have found avenues for venting the frustrations that would otherwise lead to suicide.

Confidence is often cited as a major factor in stress reduction for dentists. Those who are confident communicate this to their patients and thus have to cope with less client fear. Ultimately, it even lessens dentists' insecurities about themselves and their profession.

Operating Room Nursing: There's No Time to Panic

A career as an operating room nurse sounds exciting to many. However, it is fraught with stressors.

The intensity of the relationships within the operating room team is often cited as a high-impact pressure. If the relationship is good, the team will work well. If the relationship is bad, team members have to expend a great deal of energy in coping with the situation so the patient can still undergo a successful procedure.

Paramount to an operating room nurse's success is the ability to maintain inner control at all times. Consequently, vehicles outside the operating room must be used for venting stress. In some cases, nurses compensate by expressing anger to their peers or subordinates. In others, they might be totally in control whenever they are at work but when they go home they take out their frustrations on their families.

The multiphasic duties involved in this profession create unique conflicts. In one situation, the operating room nurse might need to be social and reassuring with a patient. A few minutes later, however, antithetical behavior is demanded; skills required at that point are anti-social and specifically medical.

The anticipation of crisis is a pressure always present with operating room nurses. While more than half of all operations go just as the textbook says they should, unexpected crises can arise in even the most routine surgery. Therefore nurses have to be constantly geared up to act whenever a lifesaving situation arises.

The accountability of operating room nurses is especially high. They are responsible for using correct technical procedures in surgery, but they may also be accountable for the training of an individual. Therefore their responsibilities involve controllable factors only part of the time.

Physical stresses are an almost subconscious part of a nurse's routine. Most nurses report that involvement in a surgical operation is so intense that they don't even think of hunger, exhaustion, or other bodily needs. Most nurses will remain at their stations through entire operations, even those which are so complex they might involve as much as a day.

Every procedure an operating room nurse is involved in is potentially lifesaving. It is also potentially life-threatening. Consequently, the members of this profession live continually under a cloud of anxiety that is both anticipated and real.

How High Is the Stress in Your Occupation?

This questionnaire can be useful to you in determining the general level of stress inherent in your occupation. Answer yes or no to each statement.

YES   NO

1. ____ ____ Does your work involve responsibility for people? Or does it involve responsibility for things which affect the well-being of others?

2. ____ ____ Is there continual pressure in your work?

3. ____ ____ Does your work involve substantial interfacing with the public?

4. ____ ____ In your occupation, is there frequent absenteeism or leave of absence due to medical problems?

5. ____ ____ Are your insurance premiums higher than those for other occupations?

6. ____ ____ Are you usually exhausted or fatigued at the end of each working day?

7. ____ ____ Could a mistake in your work critically affect the lives of others?

8. ____ ____ Does your work consist primarily of things which cannot be predicted or controlled on a day-to-day basis?

9. ____ ____ In your line of work, is it typical to find heavy drinking or marital problems?

10. ____ ____ Do you usually feel keyed up when you are off the job as well as when you are at work?

11. ____ ____ Do you have problems sleeping at night?

12. ____ ____ Do little things irritate or annoy you?

═══ ═══ TOTAL

If you answered yes to nine or more questions, your occupation is highly stressful. You must therefore consciously and consistently find ways to release that pressure so it won't affect your health.

If you answered six to eight questions affirmatively, stress in your occupation is moderate to high. The extent to which it affects you will depend upon your personal reaction to the stressor. It will also depend upon the coping skills you have learned.

A total of five questions answered affirmatively indicates that certain aspects of your work may contain stress. These will be manageable once you pinpoint the areas of difficulty.

If your occupation is stressful, the relaxation exercise

which follows may help you control the effects of that stress.

An Exercise to Reduce Stress in Any Occupation

Most people, regardless of their occupation, have a difficult time turning from job-related mental stress once they leave work, especially if they have had a particularly grueling day. The following technique may be useful in those situations.

This Mind Clearing Exercise will help you neutralize the myriad thoughts, worries, and aggravations of your day so they won't drain your energy or affect your decision-making ability. After just ten minutes of practice you should feel refreshed and revitalized.

MIND CLEARING EXERCISE

Find a comfortable position in your chair or bed. Close your eyes and try to relax. Breathe deeply two or three times. Now, take another deep breath, hold it a few seconds, and then slowly let it out. Mentally say to yourself that you are becoming calm, you are relaxing, and you are at peace.

Let all your muscles go as loose and limp as you possibly can. Start with your right leg and gradually move to every other part of your body. First tighten your muscles, then deliberately relax them.

Eventually your arms and legs may start to feel heavy.

Or they may instead feel unusually light. Whatever feeling you have, take time to experience the sensation of it fully.

Now pretend you are walking through the forest. As you visualize the setting, feel the grass beneath you getting softer and softer. Soon you reach the end of a long, cool trail and find that it leads into a beautiful, room-size opening. The opening is filled with scented wild flowers, and it is completely yours to enjoy. No other person knows about your forest room. Remember that you have this room available to you whenever you want to come to it. Spend at least two or three more minutes in your forest room.

While relaxing deeply in your special retreat, notice each breath you take. You will find that you become more comfortable and relaxed with each additional breath. Breathe slowly and deeply.

When you have had a while in which to experience fully the relaxation of your forest room, or whatever other refuge you visualize, make a suggestion to yourself of whatever you want to accomplish that day. Stay in your state of relaxation while you decide how you want to accomplish it. Then slowly visualize yourself walking back out of the forest. You will feel rested and refreshed, wide awake and calm.

SUMMARY

American society is saturated with individuals who have stressful careers. Some have more pressure than others. Occasionally stress is harmful to them not so much because of the quality of it as because of the quantity of it. Brief, intense stress is not nearly as deadly as that which is prolonged.

No matter what the career or what the amount of stress, coping facilities can compensate for the tension and even reduce the potential for physical damage. Regardless of personalities, this alternative is available to every individual who will seek it.

BIBLIOGRAPHY

STRESS AND JOB PERFORMANCE

Berlyne, Daniel, "Conflict and Arousal," *Scientific American,* August 1966, Vol. 215, No. 2, pp. 82–87.

Chase, Daniel, "Sources of Mental Stress and How to Avoid Them," *Supervisory Management,* November 1972, pp. 33–35.

Horn, Jack, "Bored to Sickness," *Psychology Today,* November 1975, p. 92.

———, "Peak Performance—The Factors That Produce It," *Psychology Today,* February 1978, p. 110.

Huddle, Donald, "How to Live with Stress on the Job," *Personnel,* March–April 1967, pp. 31–37.

Kerner, Fred, *Stress and Your Heart* (New York: Hawthorne Books, 1961), p. 73.

Levine, Seymour, "Stress and Behavior," *Scientific American,* January 1971, pp. 13–18.

Meglino, Bruce, "Stress and Performance, Are They Always Incompatible?" *Supervisory Management,* March 1977, pp. 3–13.

———, "Stress and Performance: Implications for Organizational Policies," *Supervisory Management,* April 1977, pp. 25–26.

ORGANIZATIONAL STRESS

Alander, Ross P., and Campbell, Thomas J., "An Evaluative Study of an Alcohol and Drug Recovery Program," *Human Resource Management,* Vol. 14, No. 1.

"Cracking Under Stress: How Executives Learn to Cope," *U.S. News & World Report,* May 10, 1976, pp. 59–61.

Levinson, Harry, "The Abrasive Personality," *Harvard Business Review,* May–June, 1978, pp. 86–94.

————, "Oedipus in the Boardroom," *Psychology Today,* December 1977, pp. 48–51.

McDonald, Alonzo, "Conflict at the Summit: A Deadly Game," *Stress, Success and Survival, Harvard Business Review,* Fall, 1978, pp. 101–10.

Moss Kanter, Rosabeth, *Men and Women of the Corporation* (New York: Basic Books, 1977).

Slobigin, Kathy, "Stress," The New York *Times Magazine,* November 20, 1977, pp. 48–50.

Smith, Lee, "Can You Cope with Stress?" *Dun's Review,* November 1975.

Torrance, Paul, "When Groups Break Down" in *Constructive Behavior: Stress, Personality and Mental Health* (Belmont, CA: Wadsworth Publishing, Inc., 1965), pp. 161–83.

Uyterhoeven, Hugo E. R., "General Managers in the Middle," *Stress, Success and Survival, Harvard Business Review,* Fall, 1978, pp. 101–10.

STRESS ON THE JOB

Cooper, Cary L., and Marshall, Judi, "Stress and Pressures Within Organizations," *Management Decision,* Vol. 13, No. 5, pp. 292–303.

Flynn, Warren R., and Stratton, William E., "Dealing with Aggressive Employee Behavior," *The Personnel Administrator,* February 1978, pp. 53–55.

French, John R., and Caplan, Robert D., "Organizational Stress and Individual Strain," in Marrow, *The Failure of Success* (New York: AMACOM, 1973).

French, J. R. P., Tupper, C. T., and Mueller, E. F., Workload of University Professors. Cooperative Research Project 2171, University of Michigan.

Kahn, R. L., Wolfe, D. M., Quinn, R. P., Snoek, J. D., and Rosenthal, R. A., "Organizational Stress," *Studies in Role Conflict and Ambiguity* (New York: John Wiley & Sons, 1964).

Kreutz, Douglas, "Change Is the Only Constant: Menninger," *Rocky Mountain News,* September 27, 1977.

Oncken, William, Jr., Wass, Donald L., "Management Time: Who's Got the Monkey?" *Harvard Business Review,* November–December 1974, pp. 75–80.

Perkins, Dr. R. D., *How to Control Your Stress: A Handbook for Stress Management* (Atlanta: Archon Press, 1976).

Peter, Laurence, and Hull, Raymond, *The Peter Principle* (New York: Bantam Books, 1969).

Renwick, Patricia A., and Lawler, Edward E., "What You Really Want from Your Job," *Psychology Today,* May 1978, pp. 53–65.

Yankelovich, Daniel, "Managing in an Age of Anxiety," *Industry Week,* October 24, 1977, pp. 52–58.

YOUR PERSONALITY—IS IT FRIEND OR FOE?

Billings, Victoria, "Risks: Why You Have to Take Them No Matter How Scared You Are," *Glamour,* September 1977, pp. 144ff.

Coopersmith, Stanley, "Studies in Self-Esteem," *Scientific American,* February 1968, pp. 216–24.

Dodson, Fitzhugh, *The You That Could Be* (Chicago: Follett Publishing Company, 1976).

Engel, Peter H., *The Overachievers* (New York: Dial Press, 1976).

Freidman, Meyer, and Rosenman, Ray, *Type-A Behavior and Your Heart* (Greenwich, Conn.: Fawcett, 1974).

Horney, Karen, *The Neurotic Personality of Our Time* (New York: W. W. Norton & Company, 1937).

Huxley, Laura Archera, *You Are Not the Target* (New York: Farrar, Straus & Giroux, Incorporated, 1963).

STRESSES AND STRAINS OF WORKING WOMEN

Bender, Marylin, "When the Woman Is Boss," *Esquire,* March 28, 1978, pp. 35–41.

Collins, Pat, "What Every Intelligent Man Should Know About Women," *Mainliner,* June 1976, pp. 22–24.

Cooney, Joan Ganz, interview, "A Woman in the Boardroom," *Harvard Business Review,* January–February 1978, pp. 77–85.

Gornick, Vivian, "Why Radcliffe Women Are Afraid of Success," The New York *Times Magazine,* January 14, 1973.

Henning, Margaret, and Jardim, Anne, "Women Executives in the Old Boy Network," *Psychology Today*, January 1977, pp. 76–81.

Horn, Jack, "Bored to Sickness," *Psychology Today*, November 1975, p. 92.

Olsen, Jack, *The Girls in the Office* (New York: Simon & Schuster, 1972).

Pogrebin, Letty Cotten, "The Working Woman—Stress on the Job," *Ladies' Home Journal*, September 1977, pp. 58–60.

Reno, Robert, "Women's Wages Fall Further Behind," *Denver Post*, August 28, 1975, p. 34.

Seidenberg, Robert, "Room at the Top for Men Only," *Corporate Wives, Corporate Casualties* (New York: AMACOM, 1973).

"Stress Has No Gender," *Business Week*, November 15, 1976, pp. 73–74.

Yorks, Lyle, "What Mother Never Told You About Life in the Corporation," *Management Review*, April 1976, pp. 13–19.

STRESSFUL OCCUPATIONS

Balanoff, Thomas, *Firefighter Mortality Rates* (Washington: International Association of Firefighters, 1976).

Gerhardt, Gary, "Emotional Violence Leads to Police Ills," *Rocky Mountain News* (Denver), December 12, 1976, p. 12.

Martindale, David, "Sweaty Palms in the Control Tower," *Psychology Today*, February 1977, pp. 71–75.

Nightingale, Earl, "Those Punctilious Young Men," from the Earl Nightingale program "Our Changing World,"

No. 3268 (Chicago: Nightingale Conant Corporation, 1972).

Operating Room Nurses (Englewood, Colorado: Association of Operating Room Nurses, Incorporated, 1973).

Reiser, Martin, "Stress, Distress and Adaptation in Police Work," *Police Chief,* January 1976, pp. 24–27.

NOTE

A kit of four cassette tapes with eight exercises on relaxation techniques and topics covered in this book is available to readers. The cassettes can be adapted to a variety of uses for individuals or professional groups, and they are a useful tool for professionals in the fields of personnel, training, education, and counseling.

For details on the tape program CORPORATE STRESS write to:

> Ventura Associates
> 101 Park Avenue
> New York, New York 10017